150 NIFTY
DISCARD

SUPER Crafts

Written by Sharon McCoy, Joanna Siebert, Cambria Cohen,
Francesca Rusackas, Andrea Urton, and Michelle Ghaffari

Illustrated by Charlene Olexiewicz, Neal Yamamoto,
and James Staunton

LOWELL HOUSE JUVENILE

LOS ANGELES

NTC/Contemporary Publishing Group

Published by Lowell House
A division of NTC/Contemporary Publishing Group, Inc.
4255 West Touhy Avenue, Lincolnwood (Chicago), Illinois 60712 U.S.A.

Managing Director and Publisher: Jack Artenstein
Director of Publishing Services: Rena Copperman
Editorial Director: Brenda Pope-Ostrow
Director of Art Production: Bret Perry
Editorial Assistant: Jacky Jabourian
Cover Photo: Ann Bogart

Lowell House books can be purchased at special discounts
when ordered in bulk for premiums and special sales.
Contact Customer Service at the address above,
or call 1-800-323-4900.

Printed and bound in the United States of America

Library of Congress Catalog Card Number: 00-131154

ISBN: 0-7373-0514-2

RCP 10 9 8 7 6 5 4 3 2 1

Friendship Crafts

NOTE: The numbered bracelet above the heading of each craft indicates the level of difficulty, 1 being the easiest, 3 being the hardest.

Contents

Introduction

"A friend is a present which you give yourself."

—Robert Louis Stevenson

Friendship: it means so many different things. Most importantly, friendship is a special bond that people have. Think of one of your good friends—that person you can laugh with or cry with, share secrets with, or just be yourself with—and what he or she means to you. That's what friendship is all about!

The crafts in this section will help you convey your feelings to the important people in your life. There are so many ideas to choose from, you're bound to find the perfect one. You can show your friends how much you appreciate them in a fun and creative way!

At the back of this section, you'll find instructions on how to host the ultimate craft party. Make one large craft together to symbolize the event, such as the Best Buddies' Bed Sheet on page 20 or the Keepsake Box on page 46 to hold all of your friendship mementos. Or have each friend make her own project—the Flashy Look-Alike Fashions on page 66 are great activities! A party is a perfect opportunity to share some giggles and get to know each other even better.

You'll also find loads of one-of-a-kind gifts to make for special friends. The Year of Fun calendar on page 70, the Do-It-Yourself Personalized Frame on page 58, and the Egg Carton Jewelry Box on page 32 are wonderful crafts you can personalize especially for any of your friends. They will be touched by all the thought that you put into the crafts. So put on your craft smock and get ready to choose the perfect projects for your pals.

Before You Begin

The helpful hints below will make your craft-building time fun and safe for all!

♥ Adult supervision is necessary for some of the crafts, so make sure one of your parents or another adult is available to help if you choose one of the projects labeled "Adult Supervision Recommended" or "Adult Supervision Required."

♥ Read all of the directions for each craft carefully before you begin to work. Make sure you have all of the supplies you'll need, then follow the steps exactly.

♥ Think about the level of difficulty (marked in the upper right-hand corner of each craft) and the amount of time you will need to complete the project. Allow yourself plenty of time to make each craft the best you can. You don't want to be rushed or too stressed!

♥ Find a place to work that is out of the way of others and gives you room to spread out. Try to pick a place that will be easy to clean up afterward, such as a table or uncarpeted floor space. Put down newspaper or cardboard, and protect your clothing when using paint or glue.

Friendship-Power Pressed Flowers

ADULT SUPERVISION RECOMMENDED

Here's an easy way to preserve flowers so they'll last as long as your friendship!

What You'll Need

- variety of flowers
- tissue
- thick telephone book
- two bricks
- tweezers
- picture frame (any size)
- glue
- large scrap of velvet or other textured material
- scissors

Directions

1. Just before you're ready to press them, gather flowers from your yard (be sure to get a parent's permission first!), or find a field of wildflowers. Since some flowers will keep their shape and color when pressed better than others, it's best to try a variety. (Hint: Yellow and orange flowers keep their colors best.)

2. Carefully blot away any excess moisture on the flowers with a tissue.

3. Starting at least 50 pages from the front of the phone book, carefully place the flowers face down, arranging them so that they do not touch each other. You may press several flowers at once by layering them throughout the book. There should be at least 50 pages between each layer of flowers.

4. Now, close the phone book and place the two bricks on top. Leave in a dry place for four weeks. And no peeking! Opening the book before the flowers have fully dried may cause them to break. After four weeks, remove the flowers carefully. They will be very fragile and may break easily, so always handle them with tweezers.

5. Now you are ready to frame them behind glass on a textured material, such as velvet. Cut the material to fill the picture part of the frame. If necessary, glue the material down to the back of the frame. Carefully lay the flowers on top of the material. Finally, put the frame and glass over the material and flowers (just as you would with a regular photograph), and you're done!

Hanging Friendship Tree

Gather all your cards and photos from your special friends, and put them center stage! This indoor friendship tree doesn't need water—just a little TLC!

What You'll Need

- child's old umbrella (a broken one works fine)
- scissors
- three to four rolls of masking tape, various colors
- several greeting cards from friends
- photographs of you and friends together (the more the better!)
- curling ribbon, various colors
- hole punch
- heavy-duty ceiling hook

Directions

1. Begin by opening up the umbrella and carefully cutting away the fabric or plastic from the metal rods. Make sure you remove all of the material so that you're left with the "skeleton" of the umbrella.

2. Next, take the colorful masking tape and wrap it around the entire length of each rod from top to bottom. Vary the colors as you go (for instance, yellow on one, red on another, and green on the next) so that all the metal is covered.

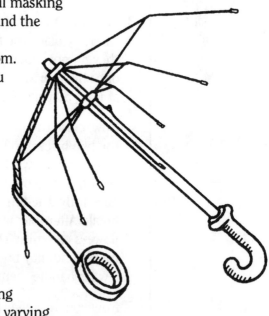

3. Now you're ready to decorate your tree! Punch one hole in the top or corner of each greeting card and picture. Cut varying lengths of curling ribbon (one for each picture and card), pull the ribbon through each hole, and tie a knot to secure. Then, tie your treasures onto the colorful ribs of the umbrella.

4. Finally, hang your umbrella upside down on a strong ceiling hook. If your ceilings are very high, tie a ribbon to the handle of the umbrella and hang it by the ribbon rather than the handle. Now all those magic moments are on display to bring you happy memories every day!

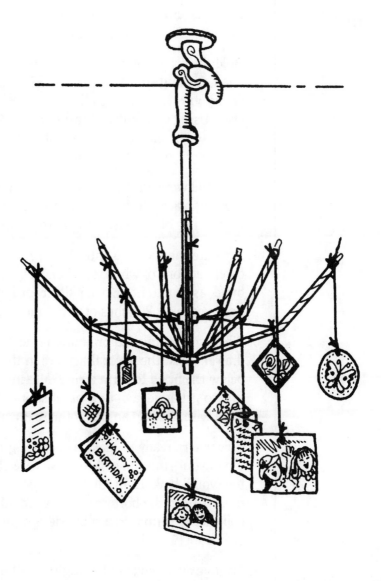

Get-Wired-on-Friendship Ring

A circle of colorful wires creates the perfect gift to say "You're the greatest" to a particular pal! Best of all, this gift is oh-so-easy on the pocketbook.

What You'll Need

- 10 inches of telephone cable, or other multiwire cable (most phone companies have telephone cable scraps that they give away for free)
- wire cutters
- ruler
- dresser drawer

Directions

1. With the wire cutters, strip away the outer cable covering from the wires. Then select six 10-inch wires from the group.

2. Hold the six wires in one hand, making sure that the ends you're holding are all even. Using your ruler, measure down 4 inches and then twist all six wires one full turn so that all the wires are fastened together at the 4-inch point.

3. Shut the wires (at the 4-inch point) in a dresser drawer to hold them in place. Or, if you have a friend around, have her hold on to the ends of the wires. Ready to begin making your ring?

4. Separate the six wires into three groups of two, then braid the three sections of wires together. (If you don't know how to braid, ask a parent or older sister for help.) Continue braiding until you have 2 inches of wire braid.

5. When you're finished braiding, remove the wires from the drawer. Twist the wires that were in the drawer to the wires below the braid to form a ring. Measure it around your finger first to get an idea of how big it should be. Then, cut off the extra wire, leaving an inch of wire on either end.

6. Now you're ready to make a cool design at the top of your ring. Take each loose wire at the top (you'll have 12 in total—six from the top, six from the bottom), and separately coil each one up into a spiral design (like a snail's shell).

7. Arrange all 12 coils in an original pattern. You can lie some flat and leave others sticking up, or arrange them in a circle.

Double Layer Daisy Pin

ADULT SUPERVISION RECOMMENDED
Pin one of these flowers onto the lapel of your fave friend, and she'll be getting a gift of friendship that goes straight to the heart!

What You'll Need

- yellow, ravel-free burlap, two 2½-inch-diameter circles
- scrap of gold burlap
- white burlap (the kind that will ravel), one 1½-inch square
- scissors
- lightweight wire
- strong glue, such as rubber cement
- ½-inch-diameter flat button
- safety pin

Directions

1. Cut two daisies from the yellow burlap, following the illustration here.

2. Put one set of petals over the other, staggering the petals.

3. With scissors, make two tiny slices through the center of both your daisies, one on top of the other, as shown.

4. Unravel the threads of the white burlap one at a time, in one direction only. You will have only loose threads left. Hold all the strips together in one hand and then, in the center of the strips, tie them with a small piece of lightweight wire (just once around will do the trick). These white threads will go in the center of your petals. Push the loose ends of the wire through the two tiny slices in the center of your daisies (one end through each slit) and pull tight. Twist the two wire ends together to keep the white threads securely fastened.

5. Cut out a ½-inch circle from the scrap of gold burlap and glue it to the button, completely covering it. Glue the button to the center of the white threads, as shown.

6. Finally, with a small safety pin, pin your daisy to your T-shirt and surprise someone special with your creation!

13

Study Buddy Book Holder

Show a friend how much you care by taking some of the pain out of homework! This super-sturdy book holder can be used time and time again.

What You'll Need

- wire coat hanger
- colorful gummed tape (gardening tape works well)
- small note card
- pen
- glue

Directions

1. Bend the wire hanger by first squeezing both arms together. Bend the two ends up and forward and fold the hook down, as shown. The hook will help support the book holder.

2. When the hanger is formed into the book holder shape, cover the wire completely with colorful gummed tape.

3. Now it's time to come up with a clever quote or message to write on a note card. A few examples are "Study with a Buddy," "Isn't it time for recess yet??," or "To study or not to study . . . that is the question!" Perhaps you and your friend have a secret saying or funny line between you. If so, this is a great place to put it in writing and keep it forever in her memory. Once you've scrawled your note, put some glue on the back of it and stick it to the center of the book holder. Your friendship and your secret saying will go down in the history books and live forever more!

"Tied" and True Friendship Sash

ADULT SUPERVISION RECOMMENDED
A colorful sash will brighten up a best buddy's wardrobe . . . and she'll remember you fondly each and every time she ties it on!

What You'll Need

- nine pieces of colored ribbon, each 6 feet long
- dresser drawer or table and masking tape
- needle
- thread
- scissors

Directions

1. To begin, hold the tops of three ribbons in one hand and measure down 3 inches. At that spot, sew the three ribbons together with a needle and thread.

2. When you've finished securing the three ribbons together, stick the ends in a drawer or tape them down to a table. Braid the entire length of the ribbons, stopping 3 inches from the end. Again, sew the three ribbons together at the 3-inch point to keep the braid from unraveling.

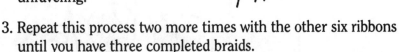

3. Repeat this process two more times with the other six ribbons until you have three completed braids.

4. Now it's time to sew all three braids together to create the sash. To do this, hold the three braids in one hand and sew them together with a needle and thread 3 inches from one end. Then, wind the three braids around one another (about eight times) and stitch them together 3 inches from the bottom.

5. Cut the ends of the ribbon diagonally to prevent fraying and unraveling. You'll create a cool fringed look!

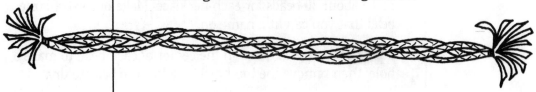

African Love Bead Necklace

ADULT SUPERVISION REQUIRED

These tribal treasures are sure to be adored by friends anywhere around the world.

What You'll Need

- 2 cups flour
- 1 cup salt
- 1 cup water
- measuring cup
- large bowl
- toothpick
- nonstick cookie sheet
- oven mitt

- red, yellow, orange, blue, green, white, brown, and black acrylic paints
- shellac
- paintbrushes
- 24 inches of colored string or thread
- sewing needle

Directions

1. With an adult's help, preheat the oven to 325 degrees. While the oven is warming up, mix the flour and salt together in a large bowl. Then add the water a little at a time, mixing it in. If the dough is still very crumbly and dry after you've added all the water, continue adding water a teaspoon at a time until it is a doughlike consistency. Depending on how many beads you plan on making, you may need to double the recipe.

2. Knead the dough thoroughly with your hands. Continue to knead the dough until it is smooth.

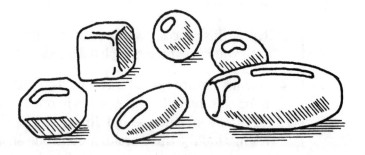

3. With the dough, begin making beads by forming small balls, about ½- to 1-inch high. Experiment with different shapes and make about 20 beads for each necklace. Make one extra-large bead that you can fit a name on.

4. Push the toothpick through the center of each bead to make a hole, then remove the toothpick to allow the bead to dry.

5. Now it's time to do the baking! Place the beads on a cookie sheet at least 1 inch apart and bake 15 to 20 minutes or until lightly browned. Using an oven mitt, remove the cookie sheet from the oven and allow the beads to cool.

6. You're ready to decorate! Paint each bead with acrylic paint. Use as many shades on each bead as you like and be creative! You can use the patterns illustrated here, or make up some of your own. Paint your friend's name or a special saying on the large bead that should fall in the center. When you're all done painting, shellac each bead and let it dry overnight.

7. With a needle, string the beads on the thread, and tie the two ends in a double knot. This ethnic-looking necklace is perfect to wear with a sweatshirt or with your favorite blouse and miniskirt.

Terrific Tees for Two

Together wherever you go! These awesome matching T-shirts will symbolize your camaraderie and show others just how much you care.

What You'll Need

- newspapers
- old clothes or paint smock
- two white, plain, oversized T-shirts
- wax paper
- acrylic paint in several of your favorite colors
- paintbrushes
- permanent ink markers

Directions

1. Slip into your old clothes or a paint smock, and head outdoors for this messy craft! Spread newspapers onto a flat surface, and lay the two T-shirts out flat, face up. Make sure you have plenty of newspapers covering the ground. Place a couple sheets of wax paper inside the shirt to prevent paint and markers from bleeding through to the other side of the shirt.

2. Dip paintbrushes into any color paint and splatter color all over the front of each one. To do this, hold the paintbrush about 3 feet over the T-shirts, and just fling your wrist. Paint will go everywhere! Use as many colors as you wish, but be sure to rinse the paintbrush with water before changing colors.

3. Let the paint dry for several hours, then turn the T-shirts over onto clean, dry newspaper. With permanent markers, write your name on the back of one T-shirt and your friend's name on the back of the other. You may want to use stencils for a neat, clean look, or write the names in your best curlicue cursive. When you're all done, you and a pal will look bold and beautiful both coming and going! (And when you are ready to wash your T-shirt, be sure to wash it by hand.)

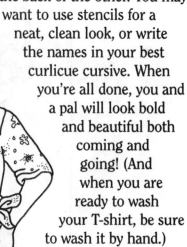

It's a Wrap!

ADULT SUPERVISION RECOMMENDED

Your buddy will be so touched when you give her a gift that's wrapped in personalized paper that she won't even care what's inside!

What You'll Need

- several feet of white butcher paper (available at craft stores or from your local supermarket)
- poster board
- pencil
- tape
- felt markers
- glitter and sequins
- rubber cement
- scissors
- colorful ribbon

Directions

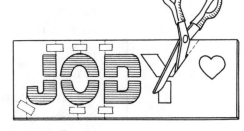

1. First, with the poster board, make a stencil that you'll repeat on the paper. In big block letters write your friend's name, ending it with a happy face, a cute heart, or other fun shape. Carefully cut out the *inside* of the letters and shape. It's okay to cut through the poster board to get to the letter—just tape it up once you've cut through it.

2. Cut the butcher paper to fit the size of the gift you'll be wrapping. On the outside of the paper (the side that will show), fill in the stencil over and over with different colored markers until the paper is filled.

3. You may want to add a special message in your own handwriting along with the stenciled name, such as "Happy Birthday, Buddy!," "Good Goin' On Your Graduation," or "Have An Awesome Holiday." When the ink is completely dry, spread clear glue on any white patches of paper, and sprinkle colorful glitter and sequins on the glue. Let it dry completely. Finally, wrap the gift and tie it all up with a ribbon!

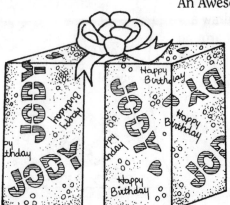

Best Buddies' Bed Sheet

The birthday girl will have sweet dreams with this super special bed sheet that she'll treasure forever.

What You'll Need

- newspapers
- white flat sheet, the same size as the birthday girl's bed
- fabric dye markers
- iron and ironing board (optional)

Directions

1. Grab a group of friends and spread out newspapers on a hard, flat surface, such as the kitchen floor. Lay the sheet over the newspapers and hand press out any creases or lumps. (If the sheet is really wrinkled, you should iron it first.)

2. Have every girl take a marker and, along the corners and edges of the sheet, scrawl a special wish that's meant exclusively for the birthday girl. Each girl can personalize her spot even more by drawing a little picture of the birthday girl doing her favorite activity (riding horses, reading books, or watching boys).

3. Then, have the girl with the prettiest handwriting write "Happy Birthday" and the date in the very center of the sheet, and draw a heart around it!

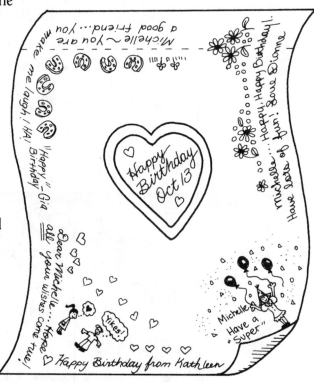

"Friends Only!" Doorknob Hanger

Adorable animal shapes are fun to paint and decorate and are the perfect addition to a buddy's bedroom.

What You'll Need

- newspapers
- 8- to 10-inch, pre-cut, wooden teddy bear, rabbit, or other animal with a hole at the top (available at craft stores)
- enamel paint, three to four colors
- paintbrushes, various sizes
- small stencils with letters or shapes, such as hearts and flowers (found at craft stores)
- thick yarn or narrow leather strip (12 to 15 inches long)

Directions

1. Spread out the newspapers over a large work surface. Choose a light-colored paint for your animal shape, and paint the front and sides all one color, using long, even strokes with one of the larger paintbrushes. Let the paint dry completely (takes about an hour), then turn over the shape and paint the back side. Let it dry as well.

2. Now comes the fun part! Choose several stencil shapes and paint them onto the animal shape. Or, just let your imagination run wild and make up your own designs to paint on the animal. Use a variety of colors for added pizazz, or match your paint colors to your friend's room for a personal touch! (Be sure to let the front dry completely before turning it over to stencil the back.)

3. When the paint has dried thoroughly, thread the yarn or leather into the hole at the top of the hanger, make a loop large enough to fit over a doorknob, and tie it into a bow. Your special gift is now ready to be received!

Sew 'n' Sleep Autographs

ADULT SUPERVISION RECOMMENDED

It's "sew" much fun to make lasting memories with your friends. Here you can make an easy pillow to take to all your slumber parties and have everyone sign.

What You'll Need

- scissors
- ruler
- light-colored solid fabric
- printed fabric
- straight pins

- needle and thread to match fabrics
- bag of polyester stuffing
- permanent ink markers, two or three colors

Directions

1. To begin your pillow, cut out two 8-inch squares from the solid material and two 12-inch squares from the printed material. The 8-inch squares should fit inside the 12-inch squares and will be the area where your friends will sign.

2. Carefully center each of the smaller squares on the larger squares and pin them into place. With a needle and thread, sew the two smaller squares on each of the larger squares. Make your stitches about ⅛ inch from the edge of each smaller square. Use small, neat stitches because they will show on your pillow.

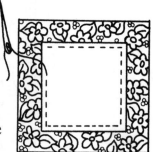

3. Now you are ready to sew the two large squares together to form the pillow. Put the two 12-inch squares together, with the two 8-inch squares facing each other (as if the pillow were inside out). Pin the edges of the two squares together with straight pins.

4. Sew around the pillow about ¼ inch from the edge, leaving 3 to 4 inches unsewn at one corner. Then turn the pillow right side out—it should look like a flat (but still beautiful!) pillow.

5. Stuff the pillow with the polyester stuffing. Because girls will be writing on this pillow, it needs to be extra stuffed to make the material as tight as possible. Once you have stuffed the pillow, close the opening by sewing up the remaining 3 to 4 inches.

6. Here comes the fun part! Take it along to your next slumber party and have all your friends sign it using a permanent marker in one area on the light-colored fabric. Once everyone has signed it, draw a line around the group of names and date it. Then, every time you go to a slumber party (or have one of your own), you can have people sign it in another area of the pillow. What a unique collector's item!

 # Valentine Goodie Box

1

ADULT SUPERVISION RECOMMENDED

Life will be sweet for a special pal when she receives a handmade box filled with Valentine's Day goodies.

What You'll Need

- solid color contact paper in pink or red, 1 yard
- round metal cookie tin
- scissors
- white household glue
- photograph of you and a friend together
- red heart stickers
- polyurethane varnish (found at craft stores)
- flat nylon brush
- homemade or store-bought heart-shaped butter cookies
- red or pink gift ribbon
- pencil
- ruler

Directions

1. Put the cookie tin on the back side of the contact paper, and trace the outline of the cookie tin on the contact paper. Cut the paper into three strips—a wide strip for the outside of the tin, a thin strip around the lid (if even necessary), and a round piece to fit on the top of the lid.

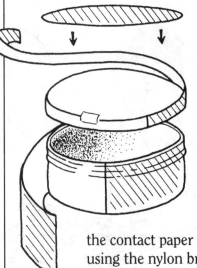

2. Carefully apply the contact paper pieces to the cookie tin. Trim off any extra paper.

3. Sparingly apply glue to the back of the picture of you and your friend. Place it on the center of the lid of the cookie tin. Add heart stickers around the photograph.

4. When the glue is dry, cover the picture, the heart stickers, and the contact paper with polyurethane varnish, using the nylon brush. Let it dry.

5. Fill the cookie tin with cookies (your friend's favorite!), and tie the ribbon around the creation. The cookies will be a quick treat, but the beautiful box will last for many happy Valentine's Days!

Baby, It's You!

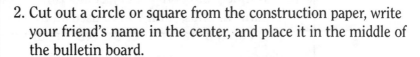

ADULT SUPERVISION RECOMMENDED

All you need to make this gift a smashing success is a close connection with your pal's parents. This is one present your friend is sure to love!

What You'll Need

- snapshots of your friend (including baby photos!), ribbons or medals that she may have won, and any other meaningful mementos
- colored construction paper

- scissors
- glue
- felt tip pen
- bulletin board
- thumbtacks

Directions

1. Lay out all the photographs and materials you have collected. Cut out borders from the construction paper for each item, then glue each item onto the paper. Write a clever saying, an amusing quote, or a personal message along the top, bottom, or side of each border.

2. Cut out a circle or square from the construction paper, write your friend's name in the center, and place it in the middle of the bulletin board.

3. Decide how you want to arrange the pieces, then tack them onto the bulletin board. Play with different combinations until you're happy with the final look!

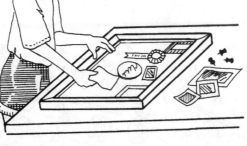

4. Arrange to take the bulletin board to your friend's house when she isn't home and hang it in her room. When she walks through the door, she'll be both surprised and delighted with this great gift!

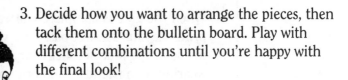

"Members Only" Bracelet

This is a perfect bracelet to make with your favorite club buddies to prove your club is the *best!*

What You'll Need

- plastic or metal slip-on bracelet (one per friend)
- several small objects related to your club (no wider than the bracelet)
- rubber cement
- red nail polish

Directions

1. First, you need to collect or make tiny symbols or objects that represent your club. For instance, if everyone in your club loves horses, make tiny horseshoes out of clay. Or, if your club is devoted to fund-raising, collect pennies to glue on your bracelet.

2. Place the objects you've chosen or made on a table with the undersides facing up, then apply rubber cement to each object. Put the first object on the center of the bracelet. Hold it in place for several minutes to make sure it sticks.

3. Continue gluing on one object at a time, working outward toward the ends, until you've used all the objects or run out of room on the bracelet. Let the bracelet dry overnight in a cool place.

4. When the glue is completely dry and the objects are secure, print the club's secret password with red nail polish on the inside of the bracelet. Let it dry. This fine jewelry is now fit for wearing with friends—and only you and the other club members know the secret password!

16 Quick 'n' Easy Ring

ADULT SUPERVISION RECOMMENDED

This traditional friendship ring takes less than five minutes to make!

What You'll Need

- plain key ring (small enough to fit around your ring finger)
- two pieces of six-ply embroidery thread, 15 inches long (two different colors—you and your best friend's favorites)
- scissors
- rubber cement

Directions

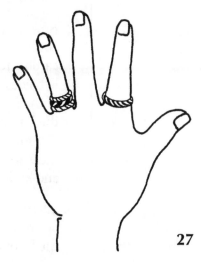

1. Lay the two pieces of thread side by side, and flatten them out with your hand. Hold the ends of the threads on the key ring with your thumb, and with the other hand, begin wrapping the strands around the ring in a slightly diagonal direction.

2. Continue wrapping the thread all the way around the key ring, keeping the threads flat against the ring. Make sure the colors are wound tightly together so that the key ring doesn't show through.

3. When you get to the end, wrap over the loose ends (the ones under your thumb) so that the strands are secure. Then wrap the threads around two to three times more and tie a small knot. To keep the ends in place, brush on a little rubber cement.

One Step Further

Because these rings are so thin, you can wear two or three on one finger. Make several rings in the same colors or use different shades for a cool effect!

ADULT SUPERVISION RECOMMENDED

Any pal would flip over this handmade diary—a special spot to scribble down secret thoughts!

What You'll Need

- two pieces of gray construction paper
- rubber cement
- scissors
- two pieces of heavy, 6-by-9-inch cardboard
- decorative piece of floral paper (like wrapping paper)
- hole punch
- ruler
- pencil
- eraser
- stack of 6-by-9-inch writing paper
- piece of string or twine, 15 inches long

Directions

1. Cut two rectangles of construction paper, each 7 inches by 10 inches. Spread the glue evenly onto the back of one of the pieces, and apply a piece of the 6-by-9-inch cardboard to the center of the paper. Wrap the ½-inch border of the paper around the sides so that the cardboard front and sides are completely covered. You may have to apply more glue to get the corners to stay down. Repeat the same process with the second piece of cardboard and construction paper. These pieces are the front and back covers of your diary.

2. Cut the decorative floral paper approximately 4 inches by 7 inches so that it fits onto the front cover as shown, then glue it into place.

3. Now it's time to punch holes in the covers of the diary. On both pieces of cardboard, measure ¾ inch from their left sides. With a ruler, draw a faint pencil line down the length of the book at the ¾-inch point. Now, measure 2 inches from the bottom of the cardboard and mark an X on the line. Measure 3 inches above that and mark another X. Finally, measure up 2 inches and draw an X. Do this on both the front and back covers.

4. Stack the two pieces of cardboard together with the X's running down the left side on the front cover. Make sure that the X's on the front cover match up exactly with the X's on the back cover.

When you're certain that you've measured correctly, punch holes over all the X's with the hole punch. Erase any visible pencil markings.

5. Place the stack of 6-by-9-inch paper between the two pieces of cardboard so that the left sides of the paper are even with the left sides of the covers.

6. Next, stick the pencil inside the holes in the cardboard, and draw three little circles onto the paper where you'll punch the holes. This step is tricky since you must hold the stack of paper and cardboard completely still as you make your markings. When your markings are accurate, punch holes in the paper. If the hole punch won't go through the whole stack, punch fewer sheets at a time, but make sure all the holes are in the same location.

7. Now you are ready to loosely string together the diary. Take your piece of twine and tie a double knot in the end. Starting from the back side, string the twine up through the bottom hole and come down through the next set of holes. Pull the twine back up through the top and final hole. Tie a double knot directly over the hole so that the string won't slip through. Don't string it too tightly; otherwise, the front cover may be difficult to open. You can leave the long pieces hanging or cut them off—it's up to you! Now, you've got a totally handmade treasure that's perfect for your pal's most personal pennings!

Friends Forever Anklet

Get your friendship started on the right foot with this adorable anklet.

What You'll Need

- three pieces of thick yarn (three different colors), 12 inches each
- tape
- five to eight small beads (with holes big enough for two pieces of yarn to fit through)
- ruler

Directions

1. Lay out the three pieces of yarn side by side. Measure down 2 inches from the top of the yarn and tie a knot. Tape the ends down on a table to keep the anklet in place while you're braiding. Begin braiding the yarn and continue for an inch.

2. Then thread two of the strands through one bead—it doesn't matter which two you thread through the bead. Braid down another inch and thread another bead through two strands. Continue this same pattern until you've braided and beaded about 6 inches of the yarn.

3. Measure the creation around your ankle to make sure it's the appropriate size. If it's too long, undo some of the braid; if it's too short, add more braiding and beads.

4. When your anklet is the correct size, remove the anklet from the table, and tie a knot at both ends to keep the yarn from coming undone. Wrap it around your ankle, and tie the ends into a bow or a loose knot. Cut off any loose ends. Now, make one for your pal, and you'll have a symbol of friendship you'll never walk away from!

19 Nature's Own Bookmark

ADULT SUPERVISION RECOMMENDED

Bring a bit of the great outdoors into your buddy's latest reading assignment with this "natural" bookmark!

What You'll Need

- construction paper
- ruler
- scissors
- pressed flowers, seeds, or leaves
- glue
- clear, self-stick paper (found at craft stores)
- hole punch
- ribbon or yarn

Directions

1. Cut a piece of construction paper about 7 inches long and 2 inches wide. Use a ruler to make the edges straight.

2. Glue the pressed flowers, seeds, or leaves onto the paper. (Learn how to make your own pressed flowers on page 3.)

3. Cut two pieces of self-stick clear paper the same size as the construction paper. Peel off the backing and put one piece on the back of the bookmark and one piece on the front so that the decorations are covered.

4. Punch a hole in the top with a hole punch. Put several strands of ribbon or yarn through the hole, and tie each one individually around the hole. What a way to mark the spot!

 # Egg Carton Jewelry Box

This box is "eggs-ceptionally" unusual and creative—and a fun way for a friend to store her treasures!

What You'll Need

- newspapers
- empty egg carton, foam or cardboard
- poster paint
- paintbrush
- photographs (optional)
- ribbon pieces and fake jewels
- 12 cotton balls
- glue

Directions

1. Spread the newspaper over a large work surface. Paint the entire egg carton with poster paint, and let it dry completely.

2. Decorate the outside of the box with ribbons and jewels. (You can even glue on pictures of you and your friends!)

3. Open up the box, and place a small amount of glue in the bottom of each egg section. Then put a cotton ball in each one. Now you've got a great resting place for jewelry!

Bloomin' Buddy Box

A healthy, thriving plant is the gift of choice since you can watch it grow along with your friendship! Plant it inside this handmade basket for a lasting (and living!) present.

What You'll Need

- newspaper
- plastic berry basket
- two yards of ½-inch-wide ribbon
- aluminum foil
- garden soil
- small plant

Directions

1. Spread the newspaper over a large work surface. Take the berry basket and weave the ribbon in and out of the basket holes as shown, leaving enough ribbon at each end so that you can tie a bow when you're finished weaving.

2. Line the entire basket (including the sides) with two layers of aluminum foil. Lay the foil so that the shiny side faces the basket holes.

3. Fill the lined basket with garden soil and then put in a small plant. Make sure you get the roots embedded deeply into the soil. Add water and get ready to make a special delivery!

One Step Further

Write a special message on a note card, punch it with a hole punch, and use some leftover ribbon to attach it to the basket. On the bottom of the note card, include simple instructions on how to care for the plant.

Heart-to-Heart Pin

Talk about wearing your heart on your sleeve! "Doughn't" ya know this heart pin is the perfect way to say "You're special" to a favorite friend?

What You'll Need

- slice of white bread
- 1 teaspoon white glue
- 1 teaspoon water
- heart-shaped cookie cutter
- safety pin
- red and white enamel paint
- paintbrush

Directions

1. First, remove the crust from the slice of bread. Then pour a teaspoon of glue and a teaspoon of water over the bread.

2. Here comes the fun part: Knead the bread between your palms until it's no longer sticky. Set the dough aside, and wash your hands thoroughly.

3. Using your hand and a flat surface, press the dough to ¼-inch thickness. Cut out a heart shape with the cookie cutter. Depending on the size of the cookie cutter, you may be able to cut out two shapes from the bread. Store the remaining dough in the refrigerator in an airtight plastic bag. It will last a couple of days.

4. Set your heart shape in a safe, dry place, and leave it to harden for 48 hours.

5. When 48 hours have passed, pinch off a pea-sized piece of the dough that was stored in the refrigerator. This piece will be used to hold the safety pin in place, which will hold your pin in place! Press the little ball of dough between your palms into a very thin oval shape, small enough to fit onto the center back of your heart.

6. Now cover one side of the oval with glue. Lay the safety pin across the center back of your heart, and lay the oval shape over one side of the safety pin as shown. Be sure that the safety pin can still open. Let it dry for several hours.

7. Once the safety pin has dried in place, paint the front of your heart red. Let the paint dry completely (about an hour or two), then paint your friend's name in white over the red. Now you've got a heartfelt gift to give that's sure to be admired by all!

One Step Further

Now that you know how to make a heart pin from bread and glue, how about trying some different shapes? Stars, flowers, four-leaf clovers, and animals are just a few of the pin shapes you can make.

Hassle-Free Headbands for Two

ADULT SUPERVISION RECOMMENDED
Get together with a friend, then put your two heads together to whip up a set of matching headbands.

What You'll Need

- 2 yards of 1½-inch velvet ribbon in your favorite color
- 12 small, fake pearls
- needle and thread (same color as the velvet)

- strong glue
- iron and ironing board
- scissors

Directions

1. You'll have enough supplies to make two headbands, so cut the 2 yards of velvet ribbon in half and split the pearls between you and your pal. Before cutting the velvet, measure it around your head by placing the ribbon under your hair at the nape of the neck and tying it into a bow at the top of your head as shown. Cut it only when you've determined how long you want the headband to be. Then untie the bow for the next step.

2. Hem under the two ends of the velvet ribbon so that they won't fray and come unraveled. Turn each side under about ¼ inch and iron into place. With the needle and thread, sew down each side, taking care to use short, neat, and accurate stitches.

3. Glue three pearls on each end of your headband, in any arrangement you like. Let the glue dry for several hours before tying on your newest creation sensation!

One Step Further

Got some extra velvet ribbon? Try using the same instructions to make matching chokers or bracelets, and you'll really double your fashion pleasure!

Forever Fresh!

These beautiful and easy-to-make pomander balls used to freshen drawers and closets have a lovely scent and will last years into your friendship.

What You'll Need

- large orange
- box of whole cloves
- velvet ribbon
- several straight pins

Directions

1. Begin sticking the cloves into the orange, putting them right next to each other. It will take patience to get the whole orange completely covered, but once you're done, the pomander ball will last for many years. And don't worry about the orange spoiling! The cloves will protect the fruit and keep it fresh.

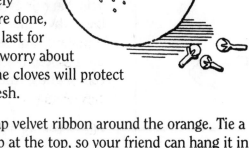

2. Wrap velvet ribbon around the orange. Tie a loop at the top, so your friend can hang it in her closet. Insert straight pins into the ribbon to keep it in place.

3. When you give the gift, let your friend know that this gift will keep moths away and is therefore perfect for putting in a drawer with wool garments.

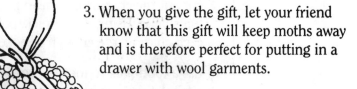

 # Official Initial Charm Bracelet

ADULT SUPERVISION REQUIRED
Your friends will be "charmed" when you suggest making these bracelets to have as keepsakes.

What You'll Need

- mixing bowl
- 1 cup cornstarch
- 1 cup salt
- cooking pot
- ½ cup water
- rolling pin
- stirring spoon
- several sharp knives
- toothpicks
- nonstick cookie sheet
- colorful tempera paints
- oven mitt
- paintbrushes
- pencil
- scissors
- shoestrings
- permanent markers
- colorful thread

Directions

1. With an adult's help, preheat the oven to 300 degrees. While the oven is heating up, make the dough for the charms. In the mixing bowl, combine the cornstarch and salt. Have an adult help you bring the water to a boil in a pot on the stove. Then lower the temperature to medium heat and slowly stir the cornstarch and salt mixture into the water. Stir the mixture until it becomes stiff. Remove the pot from the heat, and let it cool slightly. Knead the warm dough until it has a smooth consistency.

2. With a rolling pin, roll the dough to a thickness of about ⅛ inch. Divide the dough equally among your pals. Each friend will make a charm for each person in the group, including herself. Each charm should be about the size of a penny. With a knife, cut out the charms into hearts, stars, circles, or any other small, fun shapes. Using a toothpick, poke a small hole near the top of each charm large enough to poke the thread through.

3. Use a toothpick to inscribe your initials on one side and your birth date on the other. If the dough becomes crumbly, try gently smoothing it with your fingers.

4. Now you are ready to dry the charms. Put them on the cookie sheet, separated from each other. Place the cookie sheet in a 300-degree oven for about 10 to 15 minutes. Take out the cookie sheet using the oven mitt, and allow the charms to cool.

5. Give each friend the charms she made, as well as a different color of paint, so that each friend can paint them all one color. When the charms have dried, everyone keeps one of the charms and gives one to each friend in the group.

6. Now give a shoestring to each of your pals. Each girl needs to make a small loop at one end of the shoelace, by wrapping it around the pencil, then knotting it off. Make two or three tight knots so that the loop will remain tied.

7. Slip the shoelace off the pencil. Snip the plastic tip off the shoelace very close to where you tied the knots.

8. Measure the length of the bracelet by marking where the loop meets the shoelace when wrapped around your wrist.

9. Tie a knot about ½ inch from the mark on the shoelace. Keep knotting in the same spot, making the knot bigger and bigger. You'll know the knot is the right size when it can barely squeeze through the loop. This will make the bracelet easy to put on and take off. Snip the long end off. You've now created a bracelet with a built-in fastener.

10. Decorate your bracelet with markers. You can make stripes or solids, or draw rainbows or hearts—let your imagination run wild!

11. Now sew the bracelet charms on just as you would a button. Each charm represents one of your friends, and together they symbolize a whole rainbow of friendships!

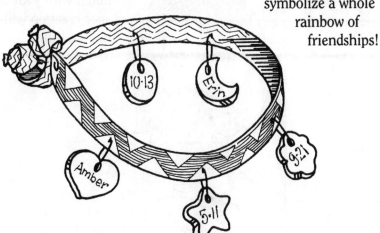

Forever Friendship Flowers

ADULT SUPERVISION RECOMMENDED

Roses and carnations that won't ever wilt, die, or fade—what a perfect way to say, "I hope our friendship blossoms forever!"

What You'll Need

- colored facial tissue
- pipe cleaners
- small pair of scissors
- lipstick

Directions

1. Hold the center of one tissue between your fingers and shake it downward. With your other hand, wind a pipe cleaner around the center of the tissue just below your fingers. The pipe cleaner will be the "stem" of the flower.

2. Using a small pair of scissors, cut the corners of the tissue to make rounded petals for roses. For carnations, snip the edge of the tissue to make fringelike petals.

3. Holding the stem, turn the tissue upward. Brush the flower petals with lipstick from about an inch inside the flower to the edge. Don't press down hard with the lipstick— brush lightly for just a touch of color.

One Step Further

Gather several shades of lipstick and make a dozen tissue flowers, then color each one a different shade. Place the flowers into a small vase, then spritz the bouquet with your favorite perfume. Your paper creation will look and smell like the real thing!

Pocket Pal File Holder

ADULT SUPERVISION RECOMMENDED

When you want to store precious memories, these secret pouches do it all!

What You'll Need

- notebook, 8½ by 11 inches, about 30 pages
- glue
- felt tip marker
- wrapping paper with print or design
- scissors
- two pieces of velvet ribbon, each 8 inches long

Directions

1. First, you want to create pockets in your notebook. Open up the book to pages 1 and 2. On the back side of page 1, apply glue in a straight line across the top, bottom, and inside of the page. Press it to the second page. When the glue dries, you'll have a "pocket" in the center. Repeat this with pages 3 and 4, 5 and 6, and so on, until you have 15 pockets in the notebook.

2. Go through the notebook and mark specific special events on each envelope. ("Disneyland Memorabilia," "12th Birthday Party," and "5th Grade Memories" are a few examples.) If you're giving this gift to a friend, label the pouches with special experiences you've shared. It's the perfect spot for storing all those outrageous memories! You can also use this book as a diary to record special events and precious moments.

3. Before you start filling up the file holder, decorate the cover and back cover. Take the wrapping paper (your choice—wild and bright, or soft and feminine!) and trace the cover and back cover onto the blank side of the paper. Then cut the two pieces out and glue them to the front and back covers. Trim off any extra paper. Finally, take the two ribbons, and glue one to the center of the back cover and the other to the center of the front cover. Tie a knot in the end of each ribbon to prevent fraying. Then use these ribbons to "tie up" your best-kept secrets!

 # Secret Message Seashell Earrings

These seashell earrings are an ocean of fun to wear and a cinch to make!

What You'll Need

- two corkscrew-type seashells, no bigger than 2 or 2½ inches (if you don't live near the ocean, craft stores carry a wide variety of seashells)
- strong glue
- tweezers
- two earring clips (available at drug, discount, and craft stores)
- two 1½-inch pieces of paper
- pen

Directions

1. Wash the seashells and dry them thoroughly. Put them on a table with the back sides facing up. Squeeze a few drops of strong-holding glue onto the backs of the shells.

2. Using the tweezers, pick up the shells one at a time and place them very gently on top of the earring clips, right in the center. Let the glue dry for several hours.

3. While the glue is drying, take the tiny pieces of paper and write secret notes for your friend's eyes (and ears!) only. Then roll them up into small, tight cylinders.

4. Once the earrings have dried, carefully stick the notes into the two shells, and give them to your friend. If the notes don't fit in the shells, make them even smaller!

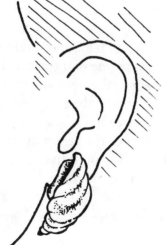

The Lantern of Friendship

Got a radiant relationship you're excited about? Let the light of friendship shine with this candle holder.

What You'll Need

- empty, smooth-sided tin can, at least 7 inches high and 4¼ inches in diameter
- paper
- pencil
- permanent marking pen
- assorted sizes of nails
- hammer
- short, thick candle
- match

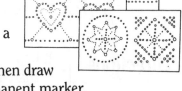

Directions

1. Clean the inside of the can and remove the paper label and glue.

2. On a scratch piece of paper, create a design that can go all around the can. Some examples are shown. Then draw the design on the can with a permanent marker.

3. Fill the can with water and put it into the freezer until the water is frozen solid. This will help the can hold its shape when you make it into a lantern.

4. Now, with the hammer and nails, punch holes in the can along the design you drew. Use an assortment of different-sized nails to enhance your design. Leave at least ¼ inch between the holes. Be sure to have an adult supervise. If the ice starts melting, put it back in the freezer for a while.

5. When you're done punching the holes, get the ice out of the can by melting it under hot water.

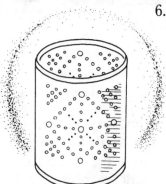

6. Dry out the can, then stick a short candle in the bottom. Make sure the candle is wide enough so that it can stand on its own. With an adult's help, light the candle, then turn down the lights and admire your beautiful lantern!

"Aloha!" Necklace

ADULT SUPERVISION RECOMMENDED

Say hello to a best buddy with this cantaloupe seed necklace, which is an awesome replica of the traditional Hawaiian friendship necklace.

What You'll Need

- seeds from four or five cantaloupes
- fine mesh sieve
- paper towels
- package of dark brown water dye
- plastic container for the dye
- hot water
- newspapers

- nylon sewing thread or a package of bead-stringing thread
- scissors
- felt marking pen
- needle
- five to seven brown, white, gray, or brightly colored beads, ¼- to ⅜-inch in diameter
- ruler

Directions

1. Remove the seeds from the cantaloupes (you and a pal can share the tasty fruit and store the remaining cantaloupe in the refrigerator!), and put the seeds into a sieve to be washed. Make sure there are no small pieces of melon remaining. Then spread the seeds out in a single layer on paper towels to dry.

2. Put 1 tablespoon of dark brown dye in a plastic container, and add 2 tablespoons of hot water. Stir the mixture to melt the dye. Then, when the dye has dissolved, add ½ cup more hot water and stir. Add ⅓ cup of seeds to the dye, stir well, and let them soak for an hour.

3. When the seeds are dark, pour the contents of the plastic container (seeds and dye) into the sieve over the sink. Rinse out the sink right away so that the dye doesn't stain it. Rinse the seeds first with hot water, then with cold water.

4. Lay down newspapers over a work surface, and lay paper towels on top of the newspaper. Put the seeds in a single layer on top of the paper towels to dry.

5. Hold the thread around your neck to measure how long you want the necklace to be. (Make sure it's long enough to go over your head.) Add 2 inches of extra thread at each end and cut.

6. Lay out the thread and mark the center with the felt marker. Plan where you want to add the beads (one for every 2 or 3 inches of cantaloupe seeds, for instance), and mark the thread with a pen. Also, mark the thread 2 inches from each end.

7. Thread the needle with the marked thread, and tie a knot 2 inches in from one end of the thread (at the pen mark). Now, push the needle through the flat center of each seed at the broadest point, and pull the thread through. Pull the seed down to the knot, and continue threading seeds. When you reach a pen mark, add a bead, then continue adding the seeds. (The seeds will hold the beads in place. If the hole of a bead is larger than the seed, then you need to find smaller beads.)

8. When you have filled the thread with seeds and beads and have reached the mark 2 inches from the end, remove the needle from the thread. Tie a knot at the 2-inch mark, then tie the two ends together in a knot. Cut off the extra thread and you're now ready to present your version of an authentic Hawaiian friendship necklace!

Keepsake Box

ADULT SUPERVISION RECOMMENDED

Need a holding place for all those special souvenirs? This box is the perfect place for storing ticket stubs, private notes, pictures, and anything else you hold near and dear to your heart!

What You'll Need

- empty shoe box with lid
- colorful wrapping paper, pages from your favorite magazine, and wallet-size pictures of you and a best buddy
- scissors
- glue
- shellac
- paintbrush

Directions

1. The design on the outside of this box should be an expression of you, so tap into your creative talents! Begin by cutting squares and rectangles of various sizes from wrapping paper and magazine pages. Cut enough to cover the outside of both the lid and the box.

2. Attach the lid to the box by slicing the two back corners of the lid up the corner creases, as shown. Then, spread glue across the entire lip of the lid, from one sliced corner to the other. Press it firmly to the shoe box. Now you should be able to lift the lid and close it like a jewelry box.

3. Glue the paper, magazine pages, and wallet-size pictures onto the box and lid. Be creative! Glue some pictures upside down, some sideways, and some overlapping others. The crazier the better! After all, it's an extension of you!

4. When the entire box and lid are covered, paint the box with shellac and let it dry completely. Give your treasure to a true friend or keep it for your own use!

Great Grains Friendship Vase

ADULT SUPERVISION REQUIRED

This unique vase deserves a place of honor in your best buddy's bedroom!

What You'll Need

- soap
- paper towels
- newspapers
- glass jar (such as a mayonnaise jar)
- 2 cups uncooked white rice
- glue stick
- rubber cement
- spray paint, in earthy colors such as rust, gold, and brown
- dried flower arrangement
- felt markers (optional)
- nail polish (optional)

Directions

1. Remove any labels from the jar and wash it with soap and water. Then dry it thoroughly with paper towels.

2. Spread newspapers on a large work surface. On one part of the newspaper, spread out the rice. With the glue stick, spread glue all over the outside of the glass jar. Work quickly so that the glue doesn't dry! Roll the glue-covered jar in the rice. Let it dry.

3. In case you missed any spots, spread another coat of glue on the jar, and roll it again in the rice, this time making sure that all areas of the jar get covered. If you are having problems getting the rice to stick in some areas, dab those places with rubber cement and then roll it in the rice. Allow it to dry.

4. With a parent's help, spray the entire jar with paint. You can also use felt markers or nail polish to create shapes or designs if you don't want to paint the whole vase one color.

5. When the paint or polish has dried, arrange a bouquet of dried flowers in the vase. Tell your friend to keep the jar dry at all times since water may loosen the glue.

 **Chain of Friendship**

ADULT SUPERVISION RECOMMENDED

This decorative paper chain will link together your group of friends in a very special way.

What You'll Need

- construction paper in assorted colors
- ruler
- scissors
- felt tip pens in assorted colors
- stapler

Directions

1. With a group of friends, measure and cut strips of construction paper 6 inches long by 2 inches wide. Each girl in the group should have the same number of strips as there are girls involved. For instance, if there are six girls at the party, each girl should have six strips.

2. When the party begins, ask each friend to write her name on all the strips of construction paper, which will later be the chain links. When everyone is done, have the girls trade their pieces of paper with each other. Each girl should end up with a paper link from each of the girls, as well as still have one of her own.

3. Now comes the fun part! Each player writes a special message to the girl whose name is on each paper link. (This means she will also be writing a message to herself.) The message should be written on the side opposite the name. It can be something the player admires about her, a special secret only for her, or an inspirational saying. Once a message has been written, "lock" the link by looping the paper into a circle and stapling the ends together. The name of the girl should be on the outside of the link.

4. When all of the links have been locked, they should be returned to their original owner (the girl whose name is written on the links). Then, with additional paper strips, each girl can put her links together, building a whole chain, as shown in the illustration on the following page.

5. Now tell each girl to take her chain home, and when she is feeling down, she can tear off one of the chains with her name on it. When she reads the special message from a good friend, it's sure to give her a lift!

One Step Further

You can make one of these chains of friendship for an extra-special friend by writing happy thoughts and encouraging words on several different links. This is one chain that won't weigh anybody down!

Pasta Necklace

Try this "tasteful" addition to your favorite friend's funky jewelry collection—a pasta necklace!

What You'll Need

- nylon fishing line or heavy string
- scissors
- pasta with holes (all different shapes, sizes, and colors)
- several wooden and gold beads
- shellac
- paintbrush

Directions

1. Hold the nylon fishing line or string around your neck to measure the appropriate length before cutting. A good length is usually 24 to 36 inches. Cut it, then lay the fishing line or string out in front of you.

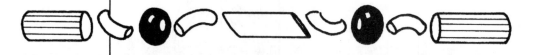

2. Set the pasta pieces you plan to use next to the fishing line or string, and arrange them in a fun pattern. Separate every third or fourth pasta piece with a bead. Play with the combinations, until you come up with a pattern that you love!

3. String on the pasta and beads in the pattern you've created. Don't forget to leave about 2 inches on either side of the line, so when you've finished stringing, you can tie the two ends of the necklace into a tight knot.

4. Paint the necklace with a thin coat of shellac to make it shine. Once one side is dry, paint the other side. After that side has dried, put it on and show it off!

One Step Further

You're sure to have leftover pasta, so if you've got some more beads, try making a bracelet or even a thin belt in the same pattern.

35 Fabulous Felt Friendship Patches

2

ADULT SUPERVISION REQUIRED

What a heart-*felt* way to say you care.

What You'll Need

- iron-on felt material, in several colors (sold at craft stores in square sheets)
- paper figures to trace, such as a bicyclist, tennis player, or cheerleader (available at craft and hobby stores)
- scissors
- felt tip pen
- iron and ironing board
- plain T-shirt

Directions

1. The first step is to choose the symbols that represent you and your friend. Since you'll be applying these to a plain T-shirt, pick several figures so that you can iron on more than one design. Come up with some of your own designs and figures.

2. Once you've decided on a theme, place the paper figure on top of the iron-on felt, and carefully trace around the edges using a felt tip pen. Use a light hand so that the ink won't spread. Cut out the designs.

3. Follow the manufacturer's instructions for using the iron-on felt when applying it to the T-shirt. Handle the iron with care—and only under the supervision of an adult. You can apply the patches on the front, on the back, or on both sleeves for extra flair. Whichever way you choose, your pal is sure to be delighted!

51

Lace Barrette

ADULT SUPERVISION RECOMMENDED
Update and upgrade a tired steel barrette for a feminine look a friend will never forget.

What You'll Need

- steel hair barrette
- rubber cement
- lace, 12 to 15 inches long
- scissors
- super glue (or other very strong glue)
- about a dozen small fake pearls

Directions

1. Open the barrette. Apply a small amount of rubber cement to the wrong side of the lace (too much glue will ruin the lace!), and apply it to the underside of the top part of the barrette.

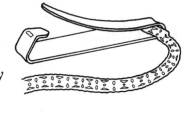

2. Wrap the lace around the length of the barrette until the top of the barrette is covered. Carefully glue down the end of the lace and let it dry.

3. Now, squeeze a dot of super glue onto each pearl, and apply them around the outside edges of the barrette, creating a border. You'll have to hold each pearl to the lace for about a minute to make sure the glue has dried. Let the glue dry overnight, and the next day, your barrette with the feminine touch is ready to be worn and adored!

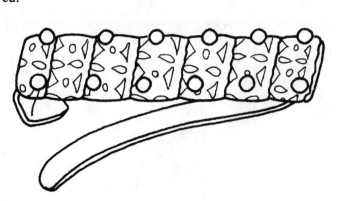

Frame Your Feelings!

ADULT SUPERVISION REQUIRED

Take a special card or poem and frame it, creating an old-fashioned, charming look.

What You'll Need

- a new or old card with a special poem or message
- scissors
- matches
- white household glue

- 5-by-7-inch matte board
- polyurethane varnish
- paintbrush
- 5-by-7-inch frame, with a stand on the back

Directions

1. Cut the card in half and keep the side with the poem or message printed on it. Ask an adult to help you burn the edges of the card with a match. *Do not do this step alone!* Over a sink, carefully burn away the outside edges of the card without burning the words. Once you light the match, be ready to blow it out immediately since all you want is a slightly burnt look around the edges.

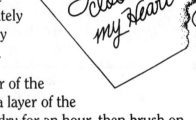

2. Glue the card onto the center of the matte board, then brush on a layer of the polyurethane varnish. Let it dry for an hour, then brush on another coat. Let it dry overnight.

3. Slip the board inside the frame, and the piece is ready for display!

One Step Further

For an even more personalized touch, sign the card before you burn the edges. Or, paint your name and your friend's name on the glass of the frame with puffy paints, which can be found in any craft store.

 # Folded
Paper Gift Box

When you give a friend a special small gift, deliver it to her in this beautiful box she'll treasure.

What You'll Need

- one sheet of medium-weight paper, 8½ inches square
- one sheet of medium-weight paper, 8¾ inches square
- markers, various colors
- stickers (optional)
- scissors
- several cotton balls
- ribbon

Directions

1. The first step is to decorate both sheets of paper however you wish. You can cover it with fun stickers or draw all sorts of fun designs on it. Another option is to use heavy wrapping paper with some kind of printed pattern.

2. Make the open box using the sheet of 8½-inch square paper. To do this, fold the paper diagonally in half, first one way and then the other. Make firm creases in the folds so that you can easily tell where the paper has been folded once you open it. Unfold the paper.

3. Fold all four corners so that they meet at the center point, then unfold the paper.

4. Now, fold each corner to the crease lines that you just made in step 3. Unfold the paper.

5. One by one, fold the corners so that they meet the crease lines on the opposite side of the square, as illustrated. Again, unfold the paper.

6. Your paper should now look like this. Cut the paper along the thick lines indicated in the illustration.

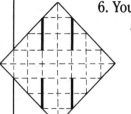

7. Fold up two opposite sides. The two corners should lay flat on the bottom of the box. Bend in the ends of the two sides to form a box.

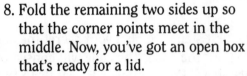

8. Fold the remaining two sides up so that the corner points meet in the middle. Now, you've got an open box that's ready for a lid.

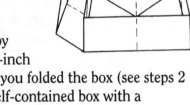

9. Now, make a lid for your box by folding the square piece of 8¾-inch paper exactly the same way as you folded the box (see steps 2 through 8). Now you have a self-contained box with a matching lid!

10. Tear apart several cotton balls to line your box with soft cotton. Your handy gift box is now ready to hold earrings, bracelets, and jewelry—just tie it up with a ribbon.

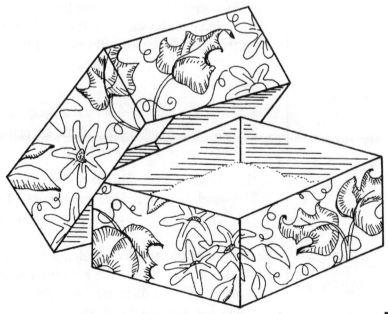

Secret Code Bracelet

All friends share classified information! Check out this cryptic way to forever document your best-kept secrets.

What You'll Need

- plastic square beads containing letters of the alphabet (found at craft stores)
- one shoelace in a bright color or neon pattern, at least 8 to 10 inches long
- several small plastic beads with holes big enough to fit the shoelace through

Directions

1. The first step is to plan your secret message so that you can spell out the code. The code will consist of the first letters of each word. For example, "Happy Birthday To A Wild Girl" would be HBTAWG, or "Janette And Jennifer Best Buds For Life" would be JAJBBFL. (Imagine how much fun it'll be to keep your message a secret while everyone tries to guess the meaning!)

2. Once you've decided on a message, string the letters in the correct order onto the shoelace. (The plastic ends of the shoelace should make it easy for you to string the beads.) Center the letters in the middle of the shoelace, then add beads in any color or pattern you choose on either side of the message. You don't need to fill the lace with beads, especially if the shoelace is a fun color.

3. When you're done stringing the beads or when you have about 2 inches left on either end of the shoelace, tie a knot at each end so that the beads won't slip off.

4. Now you're ready to tie the bracelet onto your friend's wrist. The shoelace material will easily hold a knot, but it will still be easy enough to untie when you're ready to remove the bracelet.

One Step Further

To add real pizazz to this bracelet, purchase a bracelet clasp at the craft store and tie it onto the ends instead of relying on a knot. Just make sure you measure the length of the bracelet on your friend before you add the clasp.

Buddy-Up Buttons

ADULT SUPERVISION RECOMMENDED

Turn boring buttons into beautiful ones, and make a matching set for a pal!

What You'll Need

- blouse with buttons that have loops in the back (the kinds with holes won't work!)
- scissors
- variety of fabric scraps
- fabric glue
- needle
- thread

Directions

1. Pick a blouse or shirt from your closet that you want updated, and carefully remove the buttons by snipping threads with the scissors. (Check with a parent before setting the scissors to a blouse you shouldn't!)

2. Choose the fabric to cover the buttons. You can cover each button in a different fabric, or for a more conservative look, choose the same fabric for all the buttons.

3. Lay each button facedown on the wrong side the fabric, and cut the material into a circle that's about 1½ inches wider than the button.

4. Spread the wrong side of the fabric with glue, making sure you cover the entire circle. Wrap the material around the button, pressing out any creases and making sure the fabric is flat against the button. Glue the ends to the underside of the button, but don't cover the loop. If necessary, trim off some of the excess material and threads.

5. Repeat steps 3 and 4 until you have covered all the buttons.

6. When the glue has dried on all the buttons, sew the new buttons onto your blouse. Then, make a matching set for a friend for double the fashion fun!

Do-It-Yourself Personalized Frame

ADULT SUPERVISION REQUIRED

Create an original frame that can be personalized for any special friend.

What You'll Need

- foam-core board
- X-Acto knife
- thick ribbon, lace, or other material
- fabric glue
- buttons, rhinestones, or any other odds and ends
- picture of you and a friend

Directions

1. First, you need to cut out your frame and its back. With an X-Acto knife and a parent's help, cut two foam-core rectangles that are an inch taller and wider than the picture you will be using. For instance, if the picture you want to use is 3½ by 5 inches, cut two rectangles 4½ by 6 inches.

2. With one rectangle, draw a smaller rectangle inside it that is ½ inch smaller all the way around. Then ask a parent to help you cut out the smaller rectangle. This is where your picture will fit.

3. Now you're ready to personalize your frame! Is your friend into ballet? Grab a couple yards of light pink netting. Is she into bright fun colors? Find some different colors of cellophane. With the material or ribbon you find, cut it into a long 1-inch strip. Then, start wrapping it around the rectangle with the hole, as shown. You may need to go around only once, or you may need to go around the frame a couple times to cover all white areas.

4. Glue the frame (on three sides only!) onto the second rectangle. Leave one side open to stick the picture in. Let it dry.

5. As your picture frame is drying, create a small stand so your frame can sit on a table. Simply take a piece of foam-core board, about 2 inches by 3½ inches, and on the 2-inch side, bend back ½ inch. Then glue that ½ inch to the frame, making sure that the stand will sit on a flat surface.

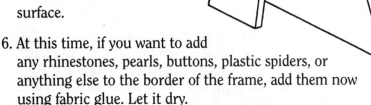

6. At this time, if you want to add any rhinestones, pearls, buttons, plastic spiders, or anything else to the border of the frame, add them now using fabric glue. Let it dry.

7. Finally, put the picture of you and your friend in the frame, and you now have a gift that is sure to warm hearts for years to come!

 # Homemade Potpourri

ADULT SUPERVISION RECOMMENDED
It makes good "scents" to give this long-lasting gift to a friend.

What You'll Need

- dried rosebuds, leaves, and colored flowers
- string
- hangers
- nylons (any color)
- scissors
- newspapers
- box of whole cloves
- ribbon

Directions

1. Pick your flowers and leaves, allowing about an inch of stem on each. With string, tie several flowers and leaves together at the stems. Continue picking plants until you have several small bunches. Hang all the bunches upside down in a dark closet to dry for two weeks. You can tie the bunches to hangers with extra string if you like.

2. In the meantime, find some old nylons you don't mind destroying. You'll want to cut one nylon square for each potpourri bag. The squares can be 4, 6, or even 8 or 10 inches on a side.

3. After two weeks, lay out some newspapers and remove the flowers and leaves. Crumble the dried plants into small pieces on the nylon squares. For each potpourri bag, add about 12 whole cloves to the dried plants, then mix it well with your fingers.

4. Bring the corners of the nylon square together to create the potpourri bag. Secure it with a ribbon by tying it first into a tight knot around the nylon, then making a pretty bow.

One Step Further

If you're pressed for time, you can buy already-dried flowers from a craft store. For a different scent, substitute your favorite perfume for the whole cloves by spritzing a generous amount onto the plants before you place the mixture in the nylon.

Best Buddy Ball

ADULT SUPERVISION RECOMMENDED

Toss this personalized ball to your best pal to send her an extra-special message!

What You'll Need

- tracing paper (or other thin paper)
- pencil
- construction paper, various colors
- markers
- scissors
- glue

Directions

1. Trace the circle shown here onto your tracing paper, then cut it out. This is your circle pattern.

2. Using the pattern, outline twenty circles on the construction paper. You can use all one color, two colors, or as many different colors as you want. Then begin folding each circle along the three dotted lines shown in the illustration.

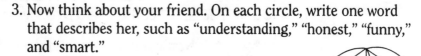

3. Now think about your friend. On each circle, write one word that describes her, such as "understanding," "honest," "funny," and "smart."

4. Begin gluing the folds of the circles together. Glue the first five circles together, joining the sides so that the five triangles point toward the center. Do the same with five other circles. You now have your top and bottom portions. Take the remaining ten circles, and glue a row around the base of the top portion. This will create a middle section to which you'll glue the base in step 6.

5. Now write an extra-special secret note to your friend. Be sure to put your name and the date on it. Then stick it inside your half-ball.

6. Finally, glue the bottom portion onto the rest of the ball. And there you have it—a unique buddy ball with a message inside!

Tic-Tac-Toe Bracelet

You'll delight the receiver of this fabulous gift, which is full of fashion and function! It's a hip bracelet that's meant to be worn anytime, but it's especially handy if you're looking for ways to pass the time. Here are the rules of the game. . . .

What You'll Need

- three felt squares, different colors
- bright yarn, 8 inches long
- Velcro strip, 5 inches long (found at any craft or sewing store)
- dice (optional)
- scissors
- rubber cement

Directions

1. First, you need to make your bracelet. Cut a bracelet out of one piece of felt that is at least 2¼ inches wide and long enough to fit around your wrist, with an inch or so left over. Cut four 2-inch pieces of yarn, then lay them out on the center of your bracelet in a tic-t   oe board pattern. Each square should be approximately ¾ inch wide. Glue the yarn pieces down.

2. Cut nine ½-inch squares of Velcro. (You'll actually have 18 squares in total, since Velcro is one piece made up of two sheets that are locked together.) Be sure that all nine squares are the same size. You can use dice to trace the shape if you don't want to draw freehand. Set the Velcro pieces aside.

3. Next cut four ½-inch squares in one of the remaining colors of felt, making sure t   the same size as the Velcro   Then cut five ½-inch squares   other remaining color of felt.

4. Now, using the rubber cement, glue the back of the rough, sharp side of each Velcro square to each felt square. Glue the backs of the corresponding Velcro squares (the softer squares) inside the tic-tac-toe board.

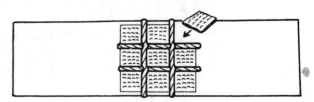

1st Color Felt

2nd Color Felt

Velcro

5. You should have a ½-inch strip of the two-sided Velcro remaining. Glue one side of the Velcro to one end of your bracelet and the second side to the other end. This will act as the fastener for the bracelet. Now you're ready to play!

How to Play

1. Find a friend to play with you. Then remove the nine felt squares from the bracelet.

2. Divide up the pieces of felt according to color (whoever goes first gets the shade with five pieces). Take turns placing squares onto the Velcro, with the aim of getting three squares in a row in any direction.

3. When you're done playing, return the nine pieces of felt to the bracelet for an armful of fashion and fun! (This bracelet comes in handy when you're waiting in line for lunch, or you need to pass a few minutes in class.)

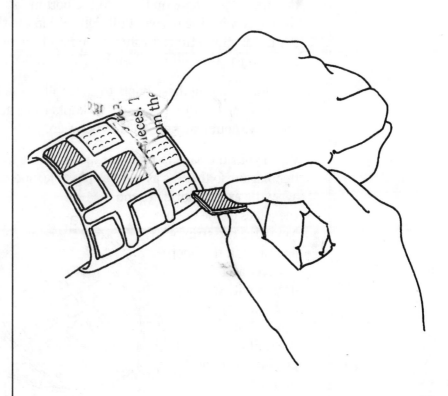

Circle of Friendship Wall Hanger

ADULT SUPERVISION RECOMMENDED

Your best friend will be "sew" delighted to hang up this handmade embroidered gift.

What You'll Need

- square of muslin material, 10 by 10 inches
- 8-inch embroidery hoop
- pencil
- needle
- embroidery thread
- scissors
- fabric glue
- strip of lace to fit around the 8-inch hoop

Directions

1. Place the muslin inside the embroidery hoop and tighten the screws so the fabric is taut across the top. Using your pencil, faintly write a message onto the fabric in block letters. (For example: BEST FRIENDS FOREVER! or YOU'RE AWESOME!)

2. Thread the needle and tie a knot at the end of the thread. Starting at the top of the first letter, come up through the bottom of the fabric with the needle. Pull tight. Wrap the thread around the needle three times as shown, and pull the needle back through the thread in the center. This is called a French knot.

3. Continue making these knots to cover all of the letters in your message. Make sure you place the knots right next to each other, without leaving spaces in between.

4. When your message is complete, position the fabric into the hoop again so that it's as tight as possible, and carefully trim away the excess fabric around the edges of the hoop. Now glue the strip of lace around the hoop to cover and decorate it. Your original artwork can be hung on the wall by placing the hoop over a nail.

Quickie Friendship Bracelet

This version of the traditional friendship bracelet will be a hands-down winner!

What You'll Need

- nine pieces of embroidery thread in three different shades, each about 9 to 10 inches long
- a knotting surface, like a book or table
- masking tape

Directions

1. First, group the nine pieces of embroidery thread together. Tie an overhand knot (illustrated here) about 2 inches from the end of the strands and tape the strands down on a book or table.

2. Take the first three pieces of the same color thread, and braid down to the bottom leaving a 1-inch tail. Repeat the process with the other two sets of embroidery thread. When you're finished with this step, you'll have three braids.

3. Now, braid all three pieces into one big braid, leaving a 1-inch tail at the bottom.

4. Tie the strand with an overhand knot to keep it secure.

5. Now comes the fun part! Tie the ends of the bracelet together around your friend's wrist. May she be forever reminded of your true-blue kinship!

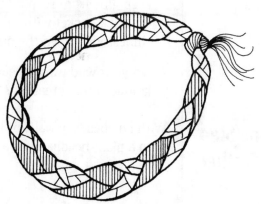

Flashy Look-Alike Fashions

Now it's a snap to double or triple up on fun fashions! Make outrageous look-alike ensembles that'll turn heads everywhere you go! This is a great project to do with a couple of friends.

What You'll Need

- newspapers
- wax paper
- dozens of fake gems and pearls, rhinestones and colored buttons
- pair of jeans and plain T-shirt for each friend
- fabric glue
- small, thin paintbrush for each friend

Directions

1. Lay out the newspapers on a clean surface to catch any glue drips, then set the T-shirts out flat. Place a couple layers of wax paper inside the shirt to prevent glue from seeping through. Choose which decorations you want to use on the T-shirt and begin putting them on the shirt. Do not do any gluing until you are finished designing. Try rhinestones around the neckline and sleeves, or a heart of pearls on the front. Anything goes, girl!

2. To fasten your creations, dip the paintbrush in the glue and apply it to the back of the decoration. Then, press it firmly onto the T-shirt and hold for a few seconds. Continue gluing until all the decorations have been placed. Set the T-shirt aside.

3. Repeat the same procedure on the jeans. (You don't need to put wax paper in the jeans—the jean material is heavy enough to keep glue from seeping through.) Try putting your initials on the back pocket with miniature buttons or running a row of rhinestones down the outside of each leg.

4. Let your wild wardrobe dry overnight. When it's time to launder these creation sensations, wash only by hand.

One Step Further

With any beads, jewels, or buttons you have left over, glue them onto a plain headband or a pair of barrettes.

 # Charming Choker

ADULT SUPERVISION RECOMMENDED

Your friend will get "all choked up" when she receives this pretty present.

What You'll Need

- strip of white lace, 1 foot long and ½ inch wide
- strip of dark green, red, or black velvet ribbon, 1 foot long and 1 inch wide
- scissors
- fabric glue
- 1-inch square of Velcro
- a small cameo brooch (found at craft stores)

Directions

1. Measure the piece of velvet to fit around your neck, then add ¾ inch to each end and cut. Measure the lace the same way and cut.

2. Apply fabric glue to the back of the lace, then place it in the center of the velvet ribbon so that the velvet shows at the top and bottom of the choker and the lace runs around the middle.

3. Glue a square of Velcro to each end of the choker so that it will fasten securely around your neck.

4. Now glue the cameo brooch in the center of the choker on top of the lace. Let it dry for several hours. You're ready to present this charming, yet easy-to-make gift!

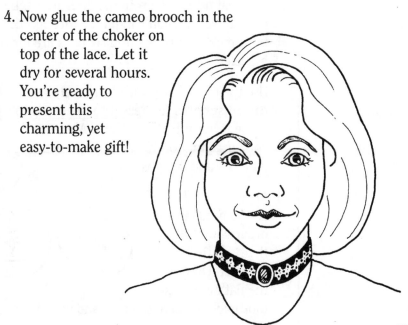

Natural Color Bead Bracelet

ADULT SUPERVISION RECOMMENDED

Create ultra-cool designs from soft bread dough, and when the dough dries, put together a masterpiece bracelet that will go down in history.

What You'll Need

- three slices of white bread, crusts removed
- 3 teaspoons white glue
- ⅛ teaspoon liquid detergent
- mixing bowl
- spoon
- old earrings and brooches to indent into the beads
- toothpicks
- spool wire
- bracelet clasp (found at craft stores)
- scissors
- varnish

Directions

1. To make the dough for the beads, crumble the bread into a bowl, then add the glue and liquid detergent. Stir the mixture with a spoon for a few seconds, then knead it with your hands. The dough will be sticky at first. When it starts to form into a ball and is no longer sticky, the dough is ready to use. Hint: If it seems too sticky even after kneading, add more crumbled bread.

2. Make little balls (about twelve balls, each ¼ inch thick) from the dough with your hands. Press down on six of the balls with your palm to make round, flatter beads. Leave them thick enough so that you can pierce through the side with a toothpick. The remaining six balls are for round beads on your bracelet.

3. Use the old jewelry with intricately carved surfaces to press into the beads to make beautiful indentations. Also, use your imagination to create your own patterns and designs.

4. Arrange the flat and round beads in the order you want them on the bracelet. On one of the flat beads, use a toothpick to carve the date and your initials in the dough.

5. Pierce holes through the side of each bead as shown. That way, the flat beads will lie flat against the wrist when strung.

6. Measure the spool wire around your wrist to see how much wire you'll need. Then, add another 2 inches on each end and cut the wire. Starting 2 inches from the end, string the beads on the spool wire. Then take your bracelet clasp and tie each of the two parts onto the two ends of the bracelet. Be sure to double-check the length of the bracelet first for a perfect fit!

7. Let the dough dry for twelve hours, then spray with varnish or lacquer for a shiny, natural look.

Year of Fun

This special gift will give your friend a whole year of fun things to do, along with happy thoughts of you.

What You'll Need

- scratch paper
- felt tip pens, various colors
- any calendar, any size
- variety of stickers

Directions

1. On scratch paper, write down activities that you and your friend enjoy doing together, as well as several activities that your friend would enjoy doing by herself. Some ideas might be: taking a bubble bath, going for a walk, playing with a pet, baking cookies, starting a journal, and boy-watching!

2. Then grab your pens and begin writing in the calendar the special activities for your friend to do throughout the year. Don't forget to include extra-fun things to do over the holidays. For instance, on July 4, you may write, "Spend the day with Lori at the park, then watch the fireworks with our favorite guys!" Write down both activities for the two of you to do together, as well as activities that she can do on her own.

3. You don't need to fill every single day, but if a week or a month is looking empty, fill it up with cute, cheery stickers or little pictures that you draw yourself.

4. Don't forget that every day you put down an activity for the two of you to do together, you need to write it down in your own calendar. Your friend will thank you for giving her such a great year to look forward to!

One Step Further

This can be done on a scaled-down version. You can give your friend a special month of fun activities, with something different to do every day of the month.

Activities for Two

"The most I can do for my friend is simply to be his friend."
—Henry David Thoreau

Whether you're spending time together on a rainy day or taking an afternoon study break, here are some terrific things you and your best friend can do together. The Study Buddy Book Holder (page 14) is fun to make and will inspire both of you to finish that weekend homework! You can write cute and encouraging messages to each other and attach them to the book holders. You might even surprise your friend by slipping a Nature's Own Bookmark (page 31) in one of her books when she's not looking!

For some really creative fun, make Terrific Tees for Two (page 18). These colorful shirts will tell everyone you're totally in sync with each other. And if you really want to get dressed up, you can make matching Hassle-Free Headbands for Two (page 36), Lace Barrettes (page 52), Charming Chokers (page 67), and Buddy-Up Buttons (page 57). Then have a funky fashion show starring the two of you!

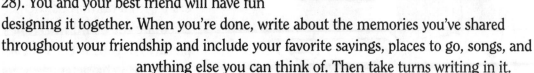

For a special keepsake you'll want to hold on to forever, do a Makin' Memories Diary (page 28). You and your best friend will have fun designing it together. When you're done, write about the memories you've shared throughout your friendship and include your favorite sayings, places to go, songs, and anything else you can think of. Then take turns writing in it. You can pass it back and forth from week to week or month to month, writing notes to each other. There is no limit to the things you can do with this personal treasure!

Special Gifts for Your Friends

"You give but little when you give of your possessions.
It is when you give of yourself that you truly give."
—Kahlil Gibran

Has one of your best friends experienced any of the following recently?
- The guy she likes has his eyes on someone else.
- She studied hard for a test, yet she scored poorly.
- Her parents are getting a divorce.
- Her favorite pet ran away.
- Her soccer team lost the championship.

Whether your friend has had any one of these things happen to her, or she's just had a string of bad days, give her a little gift to lift her spirits—made with love by you!

How about making something to show her what a terrific person you think she is? With the Best Buddy Ball (page 61) you can let her know all the things you really like and admire about her.

To show her how proud you are of her many accomplishments, you can make a Baby, It's You! wall decoration for her room (page 25). She will be honored! You can also create this wall craft with a humorous theme. Decorate the board with funny pictures of your friends, favorite comic strip characters, hilarious jokes, and whatever else you can think of that will bring a smile to your friend's face.

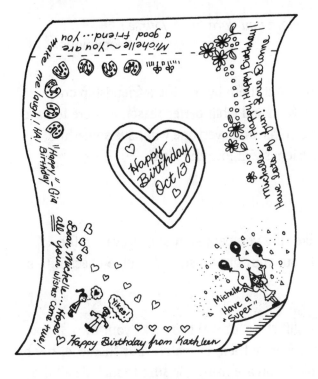

When her birthday rolls around, surprise your pal by gathering all of her friends together to make a Best Buddies' Bed Sheet (page 20). You'll have fun making it, and she'll enjoy reading what you've written. This gift will remind her always of how special she is to you and her other friends.

Just for Fun

Even gift wrapping can be personalized, so check out It's a Wrap! (page 19) and the Folded Paper Gift Box (page 54). The time and effort spent on these ideas will touch your friend as much as any gift you could give her!

Let's Party!

(A Guide to Hosting Your Own Craft Party)

"A friend is a person with whom you dare to be yourself."
—Anonymous

Show your friends how much you care about them by hosting a friendship craft party! It's a cool way to spend time together, and what better reason is there to have a party? You'll have tons of fun making crafts, and everyone will have something special to take home with them. Your friends will love the idea!

Cool Invitations

Before writing out the invitations, make sure you get parental approval on the number of guests you can invite. Write out your guest list, and double-check it to be certain you haven't forgotten anyone.

You can buy invitations from a card or gift store, or you can make your own. If you decide to design your own invitations, decorate them to match your theme, either by the crafts you are making or by the colors you are using. Be sure to include all the important information about your party, such as:

♥ Who's hosting the party
♥ What the occasion is
♥ Where it's being held (and directions if needed)
♥ When it is
♥ Any special instructions, such as things to bring, what to wear, and so on

Also ask your friends to R.S.V.P. as soon as possible and include your phone number. Let them know you'll be making crafts, so that they can wear or bring old clothing.

If you have the time, make your invitations extra-special by including a special craft item in the envelope with each invitation. Here are some ideas to get your creative juices flowing. You can choose the one that's perfect for you and your pals!

♥ For a little suspense, give each person you invite a Secret Code Bracelet (page 56) with a message on it and tell her you will reveal the hidden meaning at your party. (For instance, WHSCFTW stands for We'll Have Super-Cool Fun This Weekend.)

♥ Include a Quick 'n' Easy Ring (page 27) with each invitation. This simple yet colorful item will remind your friends that your party is coming up.

♥ Make each person a personalized Heart-to-Heart Pin (page 34) and ask her to wear it to the party. This craft is especially helpful if you are introducing new friends at your party—no need for name tags with these cool pins!

Creating the Scene

As you prepare for your party, you can cover the walls with decorations or keep the setting simple with a few strategically placed festive items. A single large craft can really jazz up the whole room! For instance, the Hanging Friendship Tree (page 10) is the perfect party piece to show off your friendships using the mementos and pictures you've collected over the years. You can even include items from the interests you

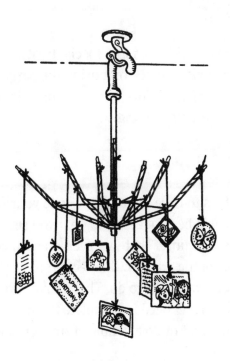

and your buddies share (such as a picture of your favorite music group or a mini soccer ball). Your friends will be delighted when they see this creative collection. When the party's over, you can hang the craft in your room.

The Lantern of Friendship on page 43 makes a pretty table centerpiece and adds a charming touch when placed in your entryway or on your porch. Your friends will be "enlightened" by your creativity!

Another great decoration is the Circle of Friendship Wall Hanger on page 64. You can embroider sentimental sayings or a special welcome to your guests. This is also a terrific keepsake.

For some colorful but simple decorations, try making a few bouquets of Forever Friendship Flowers (page 40) to brighten up the room. Put some in the bathroom, on the kitchen table, or wherever else you will be spending time.

Details, Details, Details!

No party would be complete without some special treats. Ask for a parent's help in preparing a few favorite foods to snack on during the party. And of course you'll want to play all those songs your friends love to sing along with while you are making crafts. This will really get things shaking!

Perfect Party Crafts

The purpose of the party is to have fun and celebrate your friendship, so try to relax and enjoy yourself. This will be a lot easier to do if you set up the materials you will need for your crafts ahead of time. That way everyone can concentrate on the task at hand. You can select any of the crafts in this section to work on, but decide before the party which ones you would like to do. Then make sure you have enough time and all of the materials you will need to complete them. The party can be just as fun if you focus on one super craft or do a couple of smaller ones.

♥ One idea perfect for parties is to make a friendship time capsule with the Keepsake Box on page 46. Ask your friends to bring pictures and special mementos of the times you've shared. Be sure to tell them the items are for a time capsule and won't be returned for a long, long time!

Decorate the box together, then fill it with the objects brought by everyone. Have each person write a letter to herself about what she thinks she'll be doing in the future. Drop the letters into the box, then seal it with heavy tape. Put the box in a safe place and promise to leave it untouched for the next 10 years. Make a pact with your friends to have a reunion and reveal the contents of your time capsule at that time.

Helpful Hints

To make the preparation easier, why not have your guests help out? Ask each friend to bring a different material for a craft that you will be making. Or if you are making individual crafts, such as the Flashy Look-Alike Fashions, ask each guest to bring her own item (in this case, a T-shirt). Take a close look at the list of crafts you want to do and figure out what items would be best to have your guests bring. Be specific on the invitations about what they will need and how much to buy.

♥ For a really charming keepsake, you can make bracelets, such as the Official Initial Charm Bracelet on page 38. Each person will receive her own charm bracelet to remind her of all her creative friends! She will think about friendship each time she wears it.

♥ Make a Chain of Friendship (page 48). With this craft each guest can write a personal note to her friends *and* have one to read from each of them when she's at home.

♥ The "Friends Only!" Doorknob Hanger (page 21) is a neat craft each girl can use for her bedroom. Or make an African Love Bead Necklace (page 16) that you can wear to school. Both of these projects let each person express herself as an individual while bonding with the group.

♥ If your party is a sleep-over, try this dreamy craft, Sew 'n' Sleep Autographs (page 22). You can swap stories and share secrets while everyone signs the pillow and draws little pictures. Then give the pillow to the guest of honor or the hostess as a souvenir of the evening.

♥ A nice way to capture memories from the party is to take pictures. Ask a parent to take pictures of the whole group in wacky poses, then make Do-It-Yourself Personalized Frames (page 58). As fun party favors, give each person one of the pictures for her frame to remember the evening long after the party's over.

These are just a few ideas to get you and your friends in that creative mindset. The following pages will help you with every detail of your party planning. You may want to copy these pages into a notebook or photcopy them for each party you have!

The 4-Week Party Countdown

4 WEEKS

___ Choose a theme and focus on particular crafts that would be fun to make.

___ Pick the date and time for your party.

___ Check with your parents on the date of your party and the theme.

3 WEEKS

___ Fill out the Party Specifics list and the Guest List from page 81. Have your parents check over them to make sure they are okay.

___ Fill out the Crafts list from page 82. Decide what you would like your friends to bring and who will bring specific items.

___ Buy or make your invitations. Also make any small crafts you would like to include with your invitations.

2 WEEKS

___ Deliver your invitations.

___ Complete the Decorations, Food, and Music lists on pages 81 and 82. Mark the items that you will need to buy at the store.

1 WEEK

___ Call the friends who have not R.S.V.P.'d. (If someone cannot come, you will need to buy the materials you assigned her to bring.)

___ Go shopping for the materials and other items you will need.

___ Start putting together your decorations.

THE DAY BEFORE

____ Read through the instructions of the crafts you plan to make. Double-check that you have everything you will need.

____ Call to remind your friends to bring the items for the crafts.

____ Collect old newspapers and clothing to use when making your crafts.

____ Set out the decorations and materials you will be using at your party.

____ Prepare any food that will keep overnight.

THE DAY!

____ Prepare the rest of the food and drinks.

____ Get your music set up.

____ Have fun!

AFTER THE PARTY

____ Put away leftover food and drinks.

____ Pick up all the trash.

____ Take down the decorations (move them to your room if you would like to keep them).

____ Store the extra materials to use for your next craft project.

____ Vacuum and finish cleaning up the room.

Step-by-Step to Do List

Party Specifics

Theme: _____

Date: _____

Time: _____

Place: _____

Guest List

People to invite   Invitation sent   R.S.V.P.

_____   _____   _____

_____   _____   _____

_____   _____   _____

_____   _____   _____

_____   _____   _____

Decorations

Need to make   Need to buy

_____   _____

_____   _____

_____   _____

Food

Need to make   Need to buy

_____   _____

_____   _____

_____   _____

_____   _____

Music

Songs/Groups to play   Who will bring it?

_____   _____

_____   _____

_____   _____

Crafts

Craft: _____

Materials needed   Who will bring it?

_____   _____

_____   _____

_____   _____

_____   _____

_____   _____

_____   _____

_____   _____

Craft: _____

Materials needed   Who will bring it?

_____   _____

_____   _____

_____   _____

_____   _____

_____   _____

_____   _____

_____   _____

Crafts to Make
with Things Around the House

NOTE: The number coming out of the paint tube in the upper right-hand corner of each craft indicates the level of difficulty, with 1 as the easiest and 3 as the hardest.

Contents

Introduction

Looking for the perfect handmade craft? Why not make it yourself? This section is filled with ideas for making crafts using easy-to-find materials. Each of the one-of-a-kind crafts is a blast to create! You'll find lots of tips for making each craft really special.

Before you start making any of the crafts, check out "Creating a Craft Container" on page 90. Decorating your craft container can be as much fun as doing one of the crafts! The craft container is a convenient way to store your craft supplies.

There are many crafts to choose from, so take your time as you leaf through this section. Keep in mind what items you have in your craft container, and look around your house for other materials you'll need.

If you can't find some of the craft supplies, check out "Make It Different!" on page 92. It will give you tips for adapting some of the crafts using materials you have on hand.

If you are feeling really adventurous, think about hosting a craft fair. You can raise money for a worthy cause and have tons of fun doing it! See "Hosting a Craft Fair" on page 156 for more information.

Now, get set to create!

Before You Begin

Read the following guidelines before you start doing the crafts in this section.

Some of these crafts require help or supervision from a parent or another adult. Be sure an adult is available to help if you choose a craft marked "Adult Supervision Recommended" or "Adult Supervision Required."

Think about the level of difficulty for each craft. The number in the upper right-hand corner indicates how difficult each craft is—1 is the easiest and 3 is the hardest.

Before you begin, make sure you have enough time to complete the craft you are doing. There's nothing worse than being rushed! Also, allow enough time for a thorough cleanup.

Find a good place to make the craft, especially if it might be messy. Avoid carpeted areas, and put down newspaper or cardboard when working on a table. Some projects should be done in the garage or outside. Try to find a spot where you will not disturb others.

Keep a trash container and some paper towels close at hand in case you spill.

Wear old clothing when you make crafts that might be messy.

Read all the directions carefully before you begin a craft. Gather all the supplies you will need ahead of time. Be sure you have permission to take items if they do not belong to you.

Be Safe!

Work in a well-ventilated area or wear a mask when you are using chemicals such as spray shellac, ammonia, or bleach. Call an adult immediately if you spill chemicals on your skin or clothing, or if you inhale these chemicals.

Don't pour chemicals down the sink drain. Ask an adult to find out about your city's environmental guidelines, then follow them.

Throw leftover plaster in the trash. Never throw it down the drain, as it can clog the sink.

Wash your hands after you do each craft. Also, carefully clean your work area.

Wear protective eyewear when doing a craft that requires you to chip away at plaster.

Be sure an adult is available to help if you choose to do one of the following crafts for which adult supervision is recommended or required:

Creating a Craft Container

Putting together a craft container can be lots of fun! It's also a great way to keep your supplies together, so you can grab them when you need them.

Find a box that has a lid. You can use a shoe box or another cardboard box that is a little larger. You will be able to fit more in a larger box, but don't choose one that's too big to fit in a convenient place.

Now personalize your container. Use your imagination! You can use stickers, markers, paint, and glitter to decorate it. You can create a fun collage look with some glue, wrapping paper scraps, candy wrappers, fabric scraps, magazine cutouts, post-cards, and old stamps. When you're done, let your container dry.

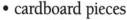

Once your container is ready, you can begin to fill it with supplies. Look around the house for these basic items, but be sure to get permission before you take anything that is not yours:

- cardboard pieces
- colored markers
- colored paper
- cotton swabs
- craft glue
- craft knife (to be used with adult supervision only)
- masking tape
- needle and thread
- newspaper
- paintbrushes
- paints

- paper plates
- pencils
- plain paper
- ruler
- sandpaper
- scissors
- spray lacquer or shellac (to be used with adult supervision only)
- stapler
- tape
- toothpicks

Keep your eyes open for household items you can reuse. Add these objects to your craft container as you find them:

- aluminum foil
- broken crayons
- buttons
- egg cartons
- fabric scraps
- glass jars
- greeting cards
- juice cans
- magazines
- milk containers (clean and empty)
- nylon stockings
- plastic baskets
- plastic lids
- sequins
- stamps
- straws
- string
- wire hangers
- yarn
- yogurt containers (clean and empty)

If you have little brothers or sisters, keep your craft container someplace where they can't reach it.

Make It Different!

Don't be discouraged if you don't have all the supplies you need to create a craft. Try making the craft using materials you *do* have. Just think of other materials that would create a similar effect. The following suggestions may give you some ideas of your own.

It's a Piñata! (page 101)

If you don't have laundry starch, try making a flour paste for your papier-mâché. Mix together ½ cup flour and ⅔ cup water in a container. Stir until the paste is sort of creamy. Use a paintbrush to cover the newspaper strips with this paste, just as you would if you were using the starch mixture.

Getting Antsy! (page 109)

If you don't have an eyedropper, you can use a drinking straw to place sugar water inside the jar. Cut off part of the straw, dip it into the sugar water, place a finger over the end of the straw, and lift the straw out of the sugar water. Hold the straw over the jar, then lift your finger off the end a few times. The sugar water will drip out of the straw and into the jar.

A Rose Is a Rose (page 141)

If you don't have any colored tissue paper, you can paint coffee filters with watercolors to create a similar look. Let the coffee filters dry completely before you start creating your flower crafts.

Walking on Eggshells (page 155)

If you don't have any eggs, try using dry pasta noodles. Wide, flat pasta works best, so crush up some lasagna noodles and get ready to paint!

What other ways can you adapt some of the crafts?

Magical Sand Art

The main ingredient in this fun craft is something the world will never run out of—sand! If you don't live near a beach, collect sand from a nearby playground or park.

What You'll Need

- 9 empty glass jars or glass bottles (with lids or caps)
- powder paints, various colors
- funnel (optional)
- sand, enough to fill the jars

Directions

1. Start by filling eight of the jars half full with sand.

2. Pick a color of powder paint and pour some of it into one of the jars. Cover the jar tightly and shake it well. The paint will color the sand.

3. Repeat Step 2 with a different color of paint and a different jar of sand. Do the same with the remaining jars, putting one color of paint in each.

4. Now get the empty jar, which can be larger than the other jars. Pick one color of sand and pour it into the empty jar to create a 1" layer. (Use the funnel if you are pouring into a bottle.)

5. Choose a different color and pour another layer on top of the previous one, creating a ½" layer. Continue with the remaining colors of sand, varying the thickness of each layer. When the jar is full, put the lid on tightly. You've got a beautiful sand "sculpture."

Home, Sweet Home

Let your imagination go wild as you build your own custom-made home!

What You'll Need

- 2 boxes of sugar cubes
- construction paper, various colors
- 12" x 12" piece of cardboard

- 10" x 10" piece of cardboard
- cellophane (or plastic wrap)
- colored paper napkins
- newspaper

- glue or rubber cement
- scissors
- thread
- tape
- sandpaper

Directions

1. First, lay down some newspaper and put the larger piece of cardboard on it. Form a rectangle out of sugar cubes in the middle of the cardboard. The rectangle should be 10 cubes long and about six cubes wide. Glue the cubes together. Now glue on a second row, then a third, building upward. Leave an open rectangle for the front door by omitting two cubes from a few rows. To make windows, just omit one or two cubes from two consecutive rows to make an open square.

2. Stop when the house is six rows high. Now add the finishing touches! To cover the windows, cut out a square of cellophane and tape it over the windows from the *inside* of the house. Cut curtains out of paper napkins. Glue them to the inside of the windows and tie them back with thread.

3. Cut a roof out of the smaller piece of cardboard and fold it in half to make an upside-down "V." Set the roof over the house and glue it in place.

4. Finally, cut a straight or curved walkway out of sandpaper and glue it down so that it leads to the front door, which you can make out of construction paper. "Landscape" your house by cutting green construction paper for the lawn, trees, and bushes!

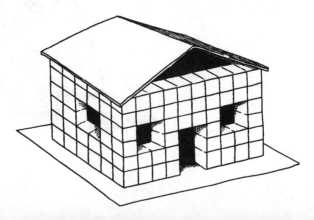

3 Works Like a Charm!

With just a few charms and simple trinkets, you can make a personal gift for your best friend or a member of your family!

What You'll Need

- small personal objects such as hair clips, buttons, perfume bottles, beads, plastic figures, erasers, rubber animals
- Popsicle® sticks (available at craft stores)
- photograph
- plastic, silver, or gold charms
- glue
- newspaper

Directions

1. To make the frame, glue 16 Popsicle sticks, edge to edge, into a flat square shape, four on each side. Overlap and glue the inner four sticks at each corner (A). Then turn the frame over and glue Popsicle sticks flat, edge to edge, to create a solid back (B).

2. Now make it charming! Lay the frame on a sheet of newspaper. Glue a charm or object onto the frame. Pick another object and glue it next to the first one.

3. Continue gluing objects. Work on alternate sides of the frame so that one side can dry while you're working on another one. Cover as much of the frame as possible.

4. Let the frame dry completely. Next, insert a photograph of the person who will receive the frame! Trim the photo if necessary, then slide it in from the side.

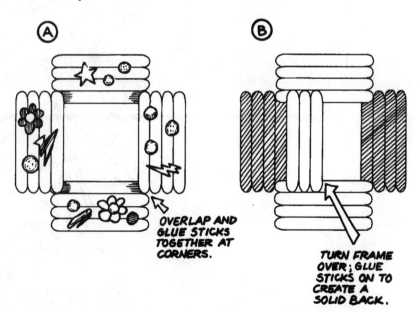

Ⓐ OVERLAP AND GLUE STICKS TOGETHER AT CORNERS.

Ⓑ TURN FRAME OVER; GLUE STICKS ON TO CREATE A SOLID BACK.

Sublime Chimes

Making beautiful music is a "breeze" with these cool wind chimes!

What You'll Need

- 2 pieces of heavy cardboard, at least 16" x 6" large
- several sheets of light cardboard
- 2 or 3 metal lids

- 3 or 4 50¢ coins
- scissors
- string
- old silverware
- tape
- ruler

- large nails
- old keys
- pencil
- glue

Directions

1. Start by making a holder for your chimes. Cut two triangles out of the heavy cardboard. The base of the triangles should be 16", and the height about 6".

2. Find the midpoint at the bottom of the first triangle and cut a 3" vertical slot. Then, from the top point of the second triangle, cut a 3" vertical slot.

3. Now use the scissors to punch a row of holes, about 1" apart, across the bottom of each triangle. The holes should be ¼" from the bottom edge.

4. Next, take the first triangle and slide it into the slot on the second triangle (A). Glue them in place if necessary.

5. Cut several 4" x 1" strips of light cardboard, one for each hole you punched in the heavy cardboard. Use the scissors to poke a hole at both ends of each strip.

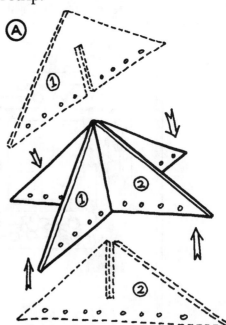

6. Now cut several 12" pieces of string. Tape the end of each string to a lid, coin, or piece of silverware. For the keys, thread the string through the hole and tie a knot. For the nails, tie the string around the nail under the head so it will hold.

7. Attach each chime to a strip of cardboard. Thread the free end of each piece of string through one hole and out the opposite hole in each strip (B).

8. Next, take the free end of each string again, put it through a hole in the heavy cardboard holder, and tie a big knot to secure it.

9. Poke a hole at the top of the cardboard holder. Thread a 12" piece of string through the hole and tie the ends together for hanging (B).

One Step Further

Next time you're at the beach, collect seashells to make into a pretty wind chime! Or try using small glass jars, such as baby food jars or pimiento jars, instead of metal objects.

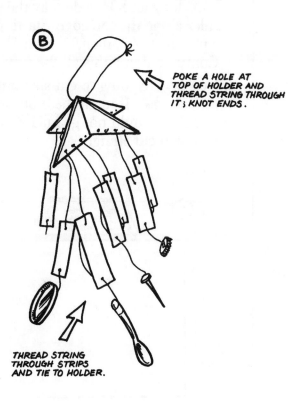

(B)

POKE A HOLE AT TOP OF HOLDER AND THREAD STRING THROUGH IT; KNOT ENDS.

THREAD STRING THROUGH STRIPS AND TIE TO HOLDER.

Zoetrope

Invented in the 1830s, the zoetrope (ZOH-uh-trohp) was an early motion-picture gadget. When it was rotated, a short movie strip came to life inside! Here's how to make a miniature version of your own.

What You'll Need

- colored pencils or markers
- black construction paper
- light cardboard
- paper cup with a flat bottom
- small bead
- scissors or craft knife
- compass
- ruler
- tape
- paper clip

Directions

1. Start by making your filmstrip. Cut a strip of cardboard 13" long and about 1½" wide. On one side of the strip, draw a moving-picture scene using the pencils or markers. You can draw a person doing cartwheels, a frog jumping, or a bird flying. When you're done, tape the ends together to form a ring, with the scene you drew on the inside of the ring.

2. To make the zoetrope, cut a strip of black construction paper 13½" long and 3" wide. Lay the strip horizontally. Place the ruler along the top edge. Starting at one end, make a mark with a pencil at $^{15}/_{16}$", then 1", then $1^{15}/_{16}$", then 2", and so on. Continue doing this all the way across the top of the strip (A).

3. Now you're going to cut slits out of the narrow areas that measure $^1/_{16}$". It might be best to use the hobby knife for this. The slits should not go farther than 1" down. Use the ruler to help you cut straight.

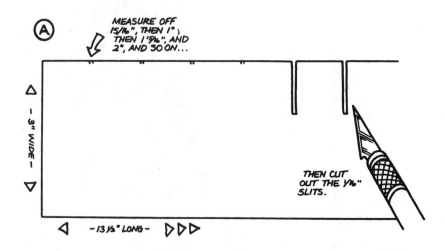

(A) MEASURE OFF 15/16", THEN 1", THEN 1 15/16", AND 2", AND SO ON...

– 3" WIDE –

THEN CUT OUT THE 1/16" SLITS.

◁ – 13½" LONG – ▷▷▷

4. To create flaps across the bottom of the strip, cut a row of notches across the bottom edge. The notches should be ¼" high. Each notch should match up with each slit above (B).

5. Fold up the flaps. Tape the ends of the strip together to form a ring. Make sure the flaps are on the inside of the ring.

6. To make the base of your zoetrope, use the compass to draw a circle with a 4¼" diameter on another piece of cardboard. Cut out the circle and drop it into the ring. The circle should rest on the flaps at the bottom of the ring. Turn the zoetrope over and tape the flaps onto the base (C). Flip the zoetrope right side up again.

7. Now set the paper cup on your work surface, bottom side up. Unbend the paper clip to form a "P" shape. Poke the stem of the clip through the center of the zoetrope base. Slide the bead onto the stem and push the clip through the center of the cup (D).

8. Drop your filmstrip ring into the zoetrope ring. Position yourself so that you are eye level with the zoetrope. Use your hand to spin the ring. Look through the slits between the black squares. You'll see a moving picture! Try creating a whole bunch of filmstrips and watch them come to life in your new zoetrope!

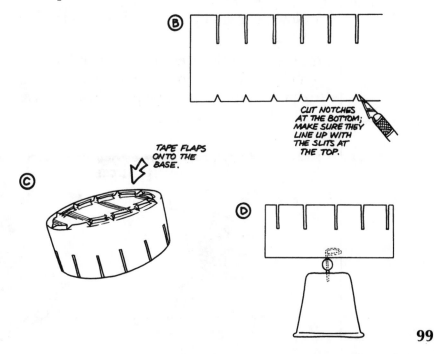

CUT NOTCHES AT THE BOTTOM; MAKE SURE THEY LINE UP WITH THE SLITS AT THE TOP.

TAPE FLAPS ONTO THE BASE.

99

Burning the Midnight Oil

ADULT SUPERVISION REQUIRED

With just a few simple tools, you can make beautiful floating lamps that will impress your friends!

What You'll Need

- wine cork
- sharp knife
- clear, shallow bowl, wineglass, or glass jar
- tweezers (optional)
- scissors
- entire wick from an old candle
- vegetable oil
- matches
- nail
- ruler
- water

Directions

1. To begin, use the knife to cut your wine cork into slices about ⅛" thick (A).
2. Carefully poke the nail through the center of each slice. Try not to crumble the cork!
3. Next, use the scissors to cut the wick into pieces ½" long.
4. String each wick piece through the hole in each cork slice. Fray each wick at one end by pulling apart the string and flattening it against the cork (A). This will prevent the wick from coming out.
5. Keep in mind that the shape of the bowl, glass, or jar you choose will make your lamp look unique. Fill the bowl, glass, or jar half full with water.
6. Now pour enough vegetable oil on top of the water to make a ½" layer.
7. Float the cork slices on the water, frayed part of the wick down, and ask an adult to light them (B). If the glass is too deep, they can hold the match in a pair of tweezers and reach down inside the glass.

Ⓐ **CUT THE CORK INTO ⅛" SLICES.**

FRAY THE END OF THE WICK.

Ⓑ

It's a Piñata!

Here's a craft that's as much fun to wreck as it is to make!

What You'll Need

- large balloon
- liquid laundry starch
- tempera paint, various colors
- tissue paper, various colors
- newspaper
- paintbrush
- assorted wrapped candies
- screw ring
- cup
- string
- masking tape
- glue
- pin or needle
- water

Directions

1. Start by blowing up the balloon and tying a knot.

2. To papier-mâché the balloon, tear a few sheets of newspaper into wide strips. Mix ⅔ starch and ⅓ water in a cup. Place a strip of newspaper over the balloon. Dip the paintbrush into the starch mixture and "paint" over the strip (A). Cover the whole balloon, but leave a hole around the knot that's big enough to fit the candy in. Let the balloon dry.

3. Pop the balloon with a pin near the knot. Shake out the balloon pieces.

4. Fill the papier-mâché balloon with candy. Cover the opening with tape.

5. Now paint your piñata in bright colors. Try gluing strips of tissue paper on each end to make your piñata look like a giant piece of wrapped candy!

6. Carefully insert the screw ring into the top of the piñata. Put a string through the ring and hang the piñata from a tree in your backyard or from a basketball hoop if you have one (B).

One Step Further

Try papier-mâchéing several balloons together in the shape of an animal. Add cardboard for ears, a starched string for a tail, and strips of tissue paper for hair.

Ⓑ

PLACE NEWSPAPER STRIPS ON BALLOON; PAINT OVER WITH STARCH MIXTURE.

Ⓐ

Marvelous Marbleized Stationery

Once you've turned plain white paper into stunning stationery, you won't want to write on anything else!

What You'll Need

- white typing paper
- disposable baking pan (larger than the paper)
- newspaper
- white envelopes
- clean rags
- water
- pencils
- enamel oil paints (2 or 3 colors)

Directions

1. First, lay some sheets of newspaper on the table. Fill the baking pan about three-quarters full with water and place it on the newspaper.

2. Now choose an oil paint. (If you use more than three colors, your stationery will look too muddy.) Dip the pointed end of a pencil into the paint, then hold the pencil over the pan and let the paint dribble into the water (A). Repeat, using a different pencil for each color.

3. Next, "pull" the paint into different shapes by lightly running the pointed end of a clean pencil (one that doesn't have paint on it) through the water. Swirl the pencil around until you have a design you like.

4. Take a sheet of paper and carefully lay it on top of the water. Wait just a few seconds, then pick up the paper by a corner and pull it out of the water (B).

(A)

5. Lay the paper, paint side up, on a clean rag and let it dry overnight. Do your writing on the white side, so the marble design is on the back.

6. No stationery set is complete without matching envelopes! You can marbleize the whole front or just the back flap. Repeat Steps 4 and 5 with a plain white envelope. If you want to marbleize only the flap, bend it up and, holding the envelope by the bottom, lay the flap on the water-and-paint mixture and pull it out.

One Step Further

Try mixing and matching colors. You can also make a marbleized journal or diary by inserting blank white sheets between two painted sheets. Make sure the painted sides face out. Punch holes in the upper and lower left-hand corners, then "bind" your diary with string or yarn.

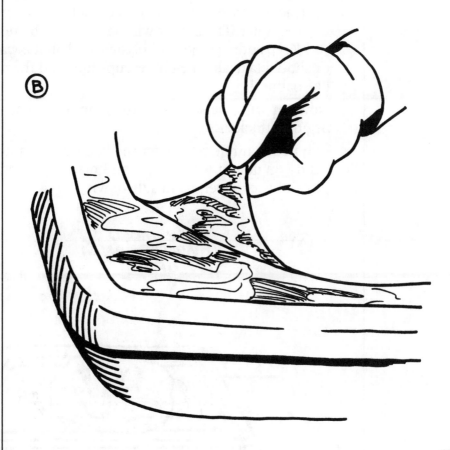

Become a Master Caster!

ADULT SUPERVISION REQUIRED

Here's how to make a perfect plaster cast of your hand. It's not as difficult as it looks!

What You'll Need

- 10-pound bag of plaster of Paris (available at hardware or paint stores)
- 2 large mixing bowls
- wooden spoon
- shallow baking pan
- petroleum jelly
- measuring cup
- wax paper
- dishwashing liquid
- water
- hammer and chisel
- pliers
- glue
- teacup
- newspaper
- paintbrush

Directions

1. First, make a mold for your cast. Lay down several sheets of newspaper to catch any plaster drippings.

2. Fill a bowl with one pint of water. Open the bag of plaster. Use the teacup to scoop out the plaster and slowly sprinkle it into the bowl of water. The plaster will start to absorb the water. Don't stir yet! Keep adding scoops of plaster until all the water is absorbed (it should take about eight teacups full) and the mixture looks like oatmeal.

3. Now stir with the spoon for three minutes. The plaster will begin to thicken.

4. Rub petroleum jelly all over the hand you're going to cast (the hand you do not write with), and place the hand on a large piece of wax paper, palm side down.

Ⓐ PLACE MOLD IN WATER, PALM SIDE UP.

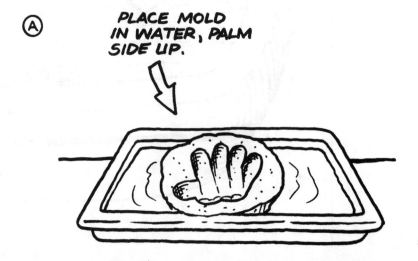

5. Have a friend or an adult use the teacup to scoop out some of the plaster mixture and pour it over your hand. Keep your hand pressed flat so no plaster gets underneath.

6. After your hand is completely covered, wait a few minutes until the plaster in the bowl thickens a bit and starts to look like sour cream. Then scoop out enough plaster to make a 1" layer on your hand. Now wait 10 more minutes while the plaster dries. Ask an adult to clean out the bowl for you before the left-over plaster dries.

7. When the plaster over your hand starts to feel warm, wiggle your fingers and slowly pull your hand out. The chunk of plaster that is left is your mold! If some of the mold breaks off when you pull out your hand, just glue the pieces back together.

8. Next, put a squirt of dishwashing liquid in another bowl and add some water to make it soapy. Then fill the shallow baking pan with water. Turn the mold over so the hand imprint is facing up. Use the paintbrush to "paint" the hand imprint with soapy water (which will make it easier to chip off the mold later). Place the mold, hand side up, in the pan of water so that only the outside of the mold gets wet (A). Hold it there for about five minutes. The outside of the mold must be completely saturated, or else it will absorb too much water out of the fresh batch of plaster that you will pour to make the cast.

9. Take out the mold and lay it on a sheet of wax paper, hand side up. Mix another batch of plaster and, when the plaster starts to get stiff, carefully pour it into the mold, filling the fingertips. Keep pouring the plaster so that it builds up to about 1" above the mold to create a base (B). Let the plaster harden; it will take at least an hour.

POUR PLASTER INTO MOLD; POUR UNTIL IT BUILDS TO 1" ABOVE THE MOLD.

Ⓑ

10. Now you need to remove the mold. You can use the pliers to break off pieces around the edge, but you'll have to use the hammer and chisel to chip away most of the mold (C). Ask an adult to help you!

11. Once the mold has been removed, soak the hand cast in some soapy water and let it dry. If you need to patch any gouges or chips, just mix a little plaster and water and fill the cracks. You've made a "hands-down" masterpiece!

One Step Further

You can shellac, varnish, or paint your plaster cast any way you want. Next time, try making a cast of your foot! Sand down the heel so that the foot stands upright with the toes pointed up. Then make another foot cast and use the two casts as bookends (or would that be foot-ends?)! Or go outside and try pouring plaster into tire tracks or animal footprints you find in the mud or dirt. When the plaster hardens, lift it up. You should get an impression of the track!

©

CAREFULLY CHIP AWAY MOLD.

Playing It Safe

You can turn an ordinary book into a special safe that only you know about!

What You'll Need

- old hardcover book
- rubber cement
- craft knife
- pencil
- ruler

Directions

1. First, find an old hardcover book, about 200 pages long, that no one wants. Open up the book to the first page.
2. Take the pencil and ruler and mark 1" in from all four sides of the page. Then connect the marks by drawing a rectangle.
3. Now use the ruler and the hobby knife to cut out the shape you just drew, leaving the 1" border.
4. Repeat Steps 2 and 3 with the remaining pages until the middle sections have all been cut out. Be patient—this may take awhile. Try cutting at least three or four pages at a time. When you're done, you should have a rectangle-shaped empty space inside the book!
5. Brush rubber cement along the four walls that line the empty space. This will hold the pages together. Let the rubber cement dry.
6. Now you have a place to hide your valuables! You can put money, secret messages, keys, or jewelry in the special compartment. When you close the book and put it on your bookshelf, no one will know it's a safe—except you!

BRUSH CEMENT ON INSIDE FOUR WALLS TO HOLD THE PAGES TOGETHER.

RUBBER CEMENT

Up, Periscope!

With this periscope, you'll be able to look over things and around corners!

What You'll Need

- tall, sturdy box, such as a liquor-bottle box or shoe box
- 2 small mirrors of the same size
- block of Styrofoam
- black paper or black marker
- scissors
- glue
- colored construction paper
- masking tape

Directions

1. First, cut off the top and bottom of the liquor-bottle box (if you use a shoe box, tape the lid closed before cutting). Then cut two holes at opposite ends of the box (A). The holes should be the same size as the mirrors.

2. Next, use black paper (or a black marker) to completely cover (or darken) the inside of the box. Don't cover the holes if you use black paper. Decorate the outside by gluing colored construction paper around it.

3. Cut two triangular wedges out of the Styrofoam. The wedges should fit into the corners of the box. Glue a mirror onto the widest side of each triangle (B).

4. Now glue each triangle into a corner of the box, opposite each hole you cut (C).

5. Hold the periscope vertically, look into the bottom hole, and you'll be able to see out the top!

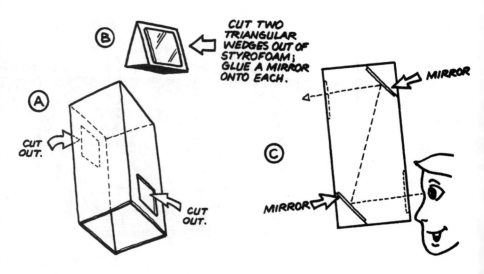

Getting Antsy!

You don't need to send away for an ant farm—you can make your very own in just a few simple steps.

What You'll Need

- large glass jar (like a peanut butter jar) with a lid
- small glass jar (like a jelly or applesauce jar)

- any size jar (to catch ants)
- soil
- sugar
- eyedropper
- drinking glass

- wooden spoon
- sand
- water
- plastic tub
- bread crumbs or food scraps

Directions

1. It's best to do this project outside so that your parents won't have to worry about ants in the house! First, mix equal parts of soil and sand in a plastic tub.

2. Take the small jar and place it upside down inside the large jar (A).

3. Now you've got to catch some ants! Fill the third jar halfway with the soil and sand mixture. Mix a little sugar and water together in the drinking glass, then stir it into the soil and sand. Lay the jar on its side. The ants will be attracted to the sugar.

4. When enough ants have crawled into the jar, pour the ants and soil into the large jar. The mixture will surround the small jar. The narrow field of vision between the large and small jars will give you a good view of the ant tunnels (B). Add more soil and sand from the tub to fill up the jar.

5. Put the lid on the large jar tightly. You don't need to poke holes in the lid. Watch the ants build their own little colony right inside the jar! Once a week, open the jar and throw in a few bread crumbs or other food scraps. Add some drops of sugar water, too, using the eyedropper.

One Step Further

Instead of ants, why not try pillbugs, earthworms (the soil must be kept damp), or any kind of ground beetle.
Large glass jars also make great homes for caterpillars, spiders, and other creepy crawlies!

The World "Accordion" to You

It looks like a cutout of your house, but . . . presto! It opens up to reveal your family tree!

What You'll Need

- several feet of continuous feed computer paper (standard 8½" x 11" sheets)
- colored construction paper
- 2 pieces of cardboard, 10" wide and 13" tall
- markers and crayons
- glue
- scissors
- pencil

Directions

1. First, tear off a set of 10 sheets of computer paper. Do not tear off each individual sheet of paper. Now trace your family tree by asking your oldest relatives about their relatives and how they came to America or to the city you grew up in (A). Write the names of your earliest ancestors on the top sheet of computer paper. Then work your way down to the present. Make sure the bottom sheet is blank. If you don't need all 10 sheets, just tear off all but one of them.

2. Once that's done, you're ready to make the "house." Draw the shape of your house on a piece of cardboard. Use up as much of the cardboard as you can.

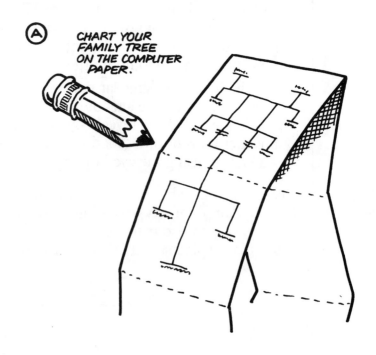

(A) CHART YOUR FAMILY TREE ON THE COMPUTER PAPER.

3. Cut the shape out and put it on the second piece of cardboard. Trace around the shape, then cut the second piece of cardboard out. The two pieces will be the front and back of your house.

4. Decorate the front of your house using the colored construction paper, markers, and crayons.

5. Now decorate the back of your house, but make sure you work on the correct side, because when both decorated sides are facing outward, the shapes should mirror each other (B). When you're done, lay the back of the house colored side down, and place the front of the house over it, colored side up.

6. Take the computer paper with your family history and put it stacked between the front and back of your house. Glue the blank side of the top sheet to the inside of the front of your house. Then glue the blank bottom sheet to the inside of the back of your house. Let the glue dry overnight. When you pull the front and back sides of the house away from each other, it should open up like an accordion (C)!

THE DECORATED BOARDS SHOULD MIRROR EACH OTHER.

Cool Crayon Art

ADULT SUPERVISION REQUIRED
Turn ordinary crayons into a beautiful wall hanging that looks like stained glass.

What You'll Need

- crayons, assorted colors
- wax paper
- scissors
- grater or pencil sharpener
- cardboard
- old pillowcase
- iron
- string
- glue
- hole punch

Directions

1. Tear off a large sheet of wax paper (about 2½' long) and lay it flat.

2. Next, make piles of crayon shavings using the grater or pencil sharpener. Spread the shavings all over the wax paper, distributing colors in whatever patterns you like. Don't put shavings near the edges.

3. Place another sheet of wax paper (the same size as the first one) over the shavings. Cover with an old pillowcase to protect the wax paper (A).

4. Now iron over the entire area of the paper. Ask an adult to help you.

5. To make the borders for your wall hanging, cut two cardboard strips. Each should be as long as the wax paper and about 2" wide. Fold the strips in half the long way.

6. Place one cardboard strip over the top end of your wall hanging so that the flaps hang over each side of the wax paper. Glue each flap down. Then glue the second strip onto the bottom of the wall hanging (B).

7. Finally, punch a hole in the top border and put a string through it. Hang your art near a window so the light can shine through!

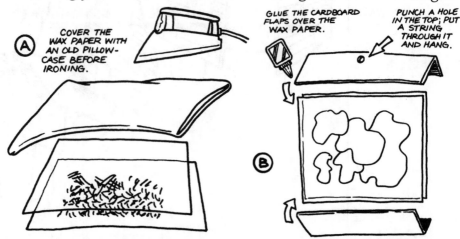

(A) COVER THE WAX PAPER WITH AN OLD PILLOWCASE BEFORE IRONING.

GLUE THE CARDBOARD FLAPS OVER THE WAX PAPER.

PUNCH A HOLE IN THE TOP; PUT A STRING THROUGH IT AND HANG.

(B)

Rolling Coasters

ADULT SUPERVISION RECOMMENDED
In just a few simple steps, you can make the coolest coasters this side of an amusement park!

What You'll Need

- lids from margarine, cottage cheese, or yogurt containers
- old greeting cards
- glue
- scissors
- pencil
- spray shellac

Directions

1. If you'd like to make a set of coasters, they should all be the same size. Start by putting a lid on top of a greeting card illustration and tracing the lid shape onto the card. Make sure you get a portion of the illustration that will look good on your coaster! Pick the prettiest or funniest part of the card.

2. Cut out the circle. Glue the circle onto the top side of the lid. Repeat with as many lids as you like. Let them dry.

3. Take the lids outside and spray them with three coats of shellac. This will make your coasters waterproof in case any drinks spill on them. Make different sets of coasters to give as gifts!

One Step Further

What else can you use besides greeting cards? How about old photos, comics, colorful magazine ads, old wallpaper, scraps of fabric, cutup book jackets, or wrapping paper? Try natural items, too, such as whole herbs or dried leaves from your backyard. You can cut or break them to fit onto the lids. As long as you shellac the coasters, they'll be protected!

TRACE LID ON CARD AND CUT OUT.

GLUE CIRCLE ON TOP OF LID.

Using Your Noodle

Here's a nifty way to "pasta" time—making cool, colorful jewelry out of all those great macaroni and pasta shapes!

What You'll Need

- assortment of dried pasta with holes, such as macaroni, wagon wheels, penne, mostaccioli, and rigatoni
- string or heavy thread
- craft paints, various colors
- scissors
- paintbrush

Directions

1. First, gather an assortment of different pasta shapes. Before you start stringing, figure out how long you'd like your piece of jewelry to be by measuring the string around your neck, wrist, ankle, and so forth.

2. Now start threading the pasta shapes in any order you like. When you're done, tie the two ends of the string into a big knot. Cut off the excess string.

3. Try it again, only this time use craft paints to paint the pasta different colors before you string them! Give this jewelry as gifts to your friends and family.

One Step Further

Mix in other colorful objects with the pasta shapes, such as buttons and various sizes of beads, both plastic and glass. These add nice variety to your pasta jewelry. Make "drops" on a necklace by stringing two or three shapes on a short piece of string and then tying it to the necklace so that it hangs down.

Eggs-ceptional!

These little egg people are so much fun to make, you'll want to create your own eggs-clusive population!

What You'll Need

- eggs
- colored construction paper
- scissors
- lace or doilies
- yarn
- fabric scraps
- any small decorative items, such as flowers, bows, and sequins
- bowl
- tape
- glue
- felt
- crayons or markers
- needle

Directions

1. See the "Walking on Eggshells" craft (p. 155) to find out how to blow out the insides of the eggs.

2. Now give your egg people character! Cut out felt or construction paper to make eyes and noses. Use the crayons or markers to add details. Add mustaches, freckles, or goatees! For hair, glue on strands of colored yarn.

3. To make a hat, cut a circle out of construction paper. Turn it into a cone shape by cutting a narrow triangle out of the circle and bringing the edges together. Decorate the hat by cutting a piece of fabric to fit over the cone shape. Glue the fabric on, then glue lace over the fabric or cut a doily to fit.

4. Finally, make a stand for your egg person by cutting a strip of construction paper about 4" long and 1" high. Glue or tape the ends together to form a circle. Rest the egg on top. Put a little bow tie or flower on the stand, or color in a tie or collar!

Candle, Candle, Burning Bright

ADULT SUPERVISION REQUIRED

Light up the night (or day!) with your own colorful homemade candles. This project can get messy, so be careful when you're handling the hot wax!

What You'll Need

- 1 pound of paraffin (available at hardware stores)
- crayons, various colors, minus paper
- 3 milk or juice cartons
- string
- 3 pencils
- newspaper
- water
- 2 tin cans, one larger than the other
- scissors
- oven mitts

Directions

1. The cartons will serve as your candle molds. Start by cutting the tops off the cartons so you have three different heights. Put newspaper under the cartons to catch any wax drippings (A).

2. Cut three pieces of string, each a few inches longer than the height of each carton. These will be your wicks.

3. Next, tie a string around the middle of a pencil. Rest the pencil on top of the carton so that the string hangs down inside the center of it (B).

4. Now take the larger tin can and fill it halfway with tap water. Set the can on the stove on low heat. Ask an adult to help you with the next few steps.

5. Cut off a chunk of paraffin (about one-quarter of the whole block) and put it into the smaller can. Now set the smaller can inside the larger can of water. If water starts getting into the smaller can, pour out some of the water.

6. Immediately put a crayon, any color, into the smaller can. The crayon will melt and color the wax.

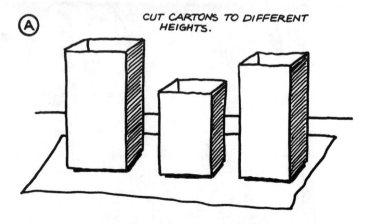

Ⓐ CUT CARTONS TO DIFFERENT HEIGHTS.

7. Once the paraffin and crayon have melted, turn off the stove. Now put on oven mitts because the can is going to be hot! Carefully take out the smaller can and slowly pour the melted wax into one of the milk cartons (C). Stop at about 1" from the top of the carton.

8. Now be patient, because you have to let the wax cool completely. Don't move or touch the carton. When the wax has hardened, tear and peel off the milk carton. Cut the string near the pencil and remove the pencil, leaving the wick behind.

9. Repeat Steps 3 through 8 for the other cartons you have—but this time use different-colored crayons!

One Step Further

Try making a candle with different-colored layers. Follow the steps above, but use a smaller chunk of paraffin. When you pour out the melted crayon and paraffin, fill the milk carton one-third of the way. Then repeat with another small chunk of paraffin and a different-colored crayon. Continue with a variety of colors until the top layer is 1" from the top of the carton. Do red and green for a Christmas candle. Or try pink, red, and purple for a Valentine's Day gift. How about black and orange for Halloween?

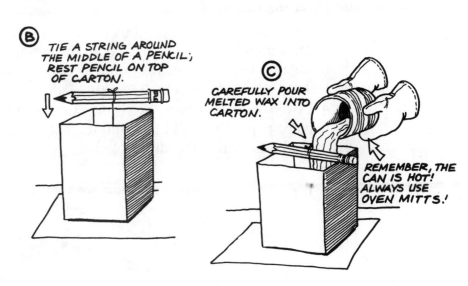

Ⓑ TIE A STRING AROUND THE MIDDLE OF A PENCIL; REST PENCIL ON TOP OF CARTON.

Ⓒ CAREFULLY POUR MELTED WAX INTO CARTON.

REMEMBER, THE CAN IS HOT! ALWAYS USE OVEN MITTS!

Which Witch?

Learn how to transform an ordinary empty bottle into a spooky witch!

What You'll Need

- empty glass bottle
- nylon stocking
- needle and thread
- orange yarn and black yarn
- cotton balls

- black tissue or crepe paper
- black construction paper
- 2 black buttons
- glue

- masking tape
- scissors
- ruler

Directions

1. To make the head, stuff a couple of handfuls of cotton balls into the foot of the stocking. Thread the needle and tie a knot at the end. You're going to make the witch's nose. Pinch the stocking between your thumb and forefinger, grabbing a wad of cotton underneath. Sew around the base of the nose, making a circle. Keep pinching the stocking and cotton while you're doing this.

2. When you're through, pull the needle and thread to tighten the stitches. The cotton will bunch up in the circle you made and stick out to form a nose. Stuff more cotton into the nose if you want. Secure your stitches by going over a previous stitch several times, making very tiny, tight stitches. Then cut off the thread.

3. Now sew on buttons for the eyes and orange yarn for the hair. Tie a knot in the stocking to hold the cotton in. Put the stocking into the mouth of the bottle so that the head rests on top. Tape the head down with masking tape.

4. Cover the witch's body by cutting a piece of black tissue or crepe paper that will fit around the bottle. Fasten the paper to the bottle with a few drops of glue.

LAY YARN INSIDE FOLD ; GLUE FLAP DOWN.

Ⓐ

5. To make the cloak, cut a 12" x 10" piece of black tissue or crepe paper. Lay the paper horizontally and fold the top edge down to make a 2" flap. Cut an 18" piece of black yarn and lay it inside the fold along the crease. Then glue down the flap (A). Now put the cloak around the bottle and tie the ends of the yarn together in front.

6. Don't forget the hat! Cut a 12" circle and a 4" circle out of black construction paper. Cut a narrow triangle out of the larger circle. Bring the edges together to form a cone, then glue them together. Glue the cone to the smaller circle (B).

7. Finally, add hands and feet by cutting them out of black construction paper. Glue the hands on the front of the cloak. Attach the feet to the bottom of the glass.

One Step Further

Here's another doll you can make. Peel an apple and carve out a simple face on one side. Stick the pointed end of a pencil into the bottom of the apple. Put the other end of the pencil into the mouth of a bottle so that the apple rests on top. Decorate the bottle by papier-mâchéing it and painting it. Then let the apple dry and watch it turn into the face of an old person. Be patient— it can take up to a month!

Ⓑ CUT OUT A 12" CIRCLE AND A 4" CIRCLE.

CUT A NARROW TRIANGLE OUT OF LARGER CIRCLE...

FORM A CONE...

THEN GLUE CONE TO 4" CIRCLE.

Ⓒ

Magic Mosaic

Everyday items take on a whole new meaning when you mix them in a mosaic!

What You'll Need

- large piece of cardboard, 2' square
- pencil
- toothpicks
- glue
- scissors
- string

- small, colorful, textured items such as broken eggshells, macaroni, rice, dried beans, dried peas, seashells, blades of grass, dried flowers, popcorn kernels, leaves, walnut shells, sunflower seeds, sequins, beads, cutup drinking straws

Directions

1. On the cardboard, draw a big picture using the pencil. This will be the outline for your mosaic. It can be a scene, an animal, a self-portrait—use your imagination.

2. Use dabs of glue to fasten toothpicks onto your pencil lines (A). You may need to bend or break the toothpicks for the short or curved lines.

3. Pick one item, such as sunflower seeds, and fill one section by gluing them down. Try to fill the entire space so no cardboard shows through.

4. Now choose another item, one with a different color and texture, and fill the section next to the one you just filled.

5. Repeat until all the sections are covered. It should look like a patchwork quilt! Let your mosaic dry overnight, then shake it gently to get rid of any loose pieces.

6. Use scissors to punch a hole in the two upper corners of the cardboard. Thread a 2½' piece of string through one hole, across the back of the mosaic, and out the other hole. Bring the two ends together and tie a knot at the top. Now your mosaic is ready to hang (B)!

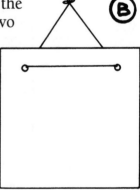

 GLUE TOOTHPICKS ONTO PENCIL OUTLINES; THEN FILL SECTIONS WITH RICE, MACARONI, OR BEANS.

Newspaper Hammock

Instead of throwing out old newspapers, why not turn them into a hammock? Here's how.

What You'll Need

- lots of newspapers
- rope or strong clothesline
- tape
- scissors
- an old bedsheet

Directions

1. Make a stack of 30 sheets of newspaper. Roll up the stack the long way to form a tight, narrow tube. Tape the tube closed.
2. Repeat step 1 until you have about 20 tubes.
3. Cut three lengths of rope or clothesline, each at least 12' long. Lay the ropes parallel to one another.
4. Now tie each tube, one by one, to the ropes. Tie over-and-under knots, leaving 2" to 3" between each tube (A). Remember to leave at least 3' at the end of each rope so you can hang up the hammock.
5. When the hammock is long enough for you to lie in, tie the ropes together at each end (B). Hang your hammock between two trees in your backyard, or ask your mom or dad to help you hang it from your patio roof! Throw an old bedsheet over the hammock so you won't get newsprint on your clothes.

One Step Further

Try making a hammock out of brown paper shopping bags. Cut the bottom off each, then cut along a side seam and spread open the bag. Stack several bags, then roll them up.

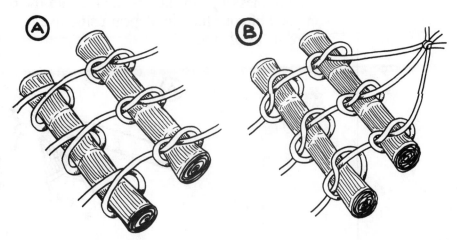

Fan-tastic!

This handmade fan is perfect for a hot summer day!

What You'll Need

- about 20 Popsicle® sticks (available at craft stores)
- light cardboard
- crayons, markers, or tempera paints, various colors
- masking tape
- scissors
- glue

Directions

1. First, cut the cardboard to make the front and back pieces of your fan. They should be the same size and shape, and the shape can be anything you want. The fan should be about 9" wide. Cut a semicircle out of the bottom of each piece.

2. Draw a design on one side of the front piece. Do the same with the back piece.

3. To make the "ribs," lay a Popsicle stick flat and put some glue on one end. Then lay the end of another Popsicle stick over the glue and press the sticks together (A). You've made one rib. Repeat until you have three ribs.

4. Lay the front piece of your fan flat, colored side down. Glue the ribs onto the plain side, bringing the three ends together to form a point as shown. Then glue one Popsicle stick to each corner, bringing their ends to a point as well (B). Let the glue dry.

5. Pick up the back piece of the fan and glue it onto the front piece, matching up the edges. The two plain sides should be facing each other. Let the glue dry.

6. Next, make the handle by laying five Popsicle sticks flat. Put a piece of masking tape across the top and the bottom. This is one half of your handle. Repeat using five more sticks and two more strips of tape.

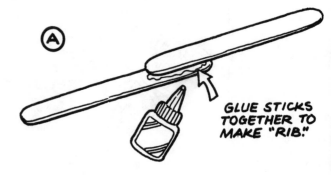

Ⓐ

GLUE STICKS TOGETHER TO MAKE "RIB."

7. Take one half of the handle and turn it over so that the tape is on the bottom. Now glue the ends of the fan ribs onto the handle.

8. Take a single Popsicle stick and break off a 2" piece. Glue this piece across the bottom of the handle half (C). Let dry.

9. Now take the other half of the handle and glue it, masking-tape side up, onto the first half (C). The fan ribs should be sandwiched between the two halves.

10. When the glue dries, wrap masking tape around the handle from top to bottom. Color the handle using crayons, markers, or paint.

One Step Further

You can decorate your fan in various fun ways. Try gluing on lace, sequins, glitter, feathers, old jewelry, fabric scraps, pieces of pretty gift wrap . . . use your imagination! You can also make a longer handle by gluing sticks end to end, like you did to make the ribs.

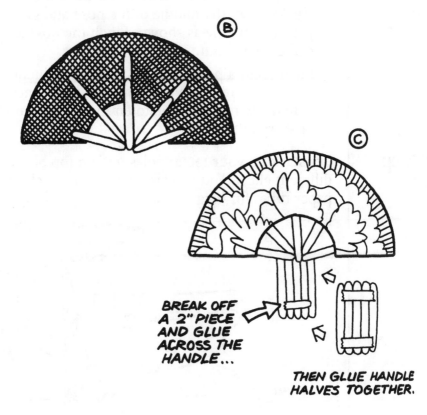

Ⓑ

Ⓒ

BREAK OFF A 2" PIECE AND GLUE ACROSS THE HANDLE...

THEN GLUE HANDLE HALVES TOGETHER.

Terrific Totems

You only need a few items to make these colorful totem poles!

What You'll Need

- empty toilet paper tubes
- crayons or markers
- colored construction paper (light colors work best)
- glue
- scissors

Directions

1. To start, cut a piece of construction paper large enough to wrap around a toilet paper tube.

2. Lay the paper flat and use the crayons or markers to draw a colorful totem face. Remember to start drawing the face in the middle of the paper. Leave space for the three-dimensional nose.

3. When you're done, wrap your totem face around the paper tube and secure it in the back with glue.

4. Now cut a nose out of construction paper. You can color the nose or just keep it the color of the construction paper. Make a crease down the middle of the nose and glue the edges onto your totem pole as shown. Pinch the nose along the crease to make it stick out.

5. Finally, cut a pair of wings out of construction paper and color them. Be sure to make the inner edge of each wing flat. Now glue the wings onto the totem pole. Make a whole set of funny or scary totems!

One Step Further

Try stacking your totem poles one on top of the other for a different effect. You can also use paper towel tubes instead of toilet paper tubes for bigger totems!

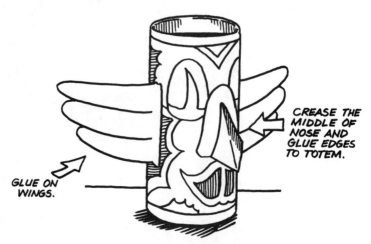

CREASE THE MIDDLE OF NOSE AND GLUE EDGES TO TOTEM.

GLUE ON WINGS.

You Scratch My Back . . .

For a quick and crazy craft, try this nifty crayon scratch art.

What You'll Need

- cardboard from a dress shirt package
- crayons, various colors, including several black crayons
- sharp objects, such as a paper clip, a ballpoint pen, a fork, a comb, scissors, a compass point, a safety pin, a coin, and a spoon

Directions

1. Start by drawing all over the entire surface of the cardboard using the crayons. Use as many colors as you like, but save the black crayons for later. The more colors you use, the better.

2. Now cover your crayon drawing with black crayon (A). Press hard! Again, cover the entire surface. Make sure you have enough black crayons!

3. Next, take the sharp objects and scratch a picture out of the black crayon (B). Scratch out a picture of your house, your pet, a castle—anything you like. Be sure to scratch just hard enough to take the black off without removing the colored crayon underneath. Use a variety of objects. A paper clip makes a thin line, while the edge of a spoon makes a wider line. Don't remove all the black crayon, though—it helps make the assortment of colors underneath shine through!

One Step Further

Here's a similar art project using black watercolor paint. Draw a picture on a piece of white paper and color it with crayons, but leave some white areas showing. Then lightly paint black watercolor over the picture. The crayon marks will "resist" the watercolor, and the paint will stay on the white areas of the paper, giving you a nice mix of paint and crayon.

Bag It!

Here's how to turn an old pair of blue jeans into a cool-looking purse, gym bag, or beach bag!

What You'll Need

- an old pair of blue jeans
- needle and thread
- heavy scissors

Directions

1. Start by cutting off the legs of the jeans about an inch below the fly. Save the legs to make into a strap.

2. If you've never sewn before, ask a parent or older brother or sister to help you out. It's very easy. Cut a long piece of thread about the length of your arms outspread. Then thread it through the needle and tie the ends together in a knot.

3. Bring together the front and back of the jeans at the bottom and sew it closed (A). Make small, tight stitches. You should go back and forth over your stitches at least twice to reinforce the bottom.

4. Next, you'll need to make a clasp to hold the top of the bag closed. Cut off the front button above the fly. Move the button to the back waistline and sew the button on the inside as shown (B). Now, to close the bag, just push the newly sewn button through the original buttonhole!

5. To make the strap, fold one of the pants legs in half the long way and sew it closed.

6. Now sew each end of the strap to the inside of the waistline (C). Sew the strap securely, otherwise it may break when your bag is full. Now you're a real blue-jean baby!

MOVE THE BUTTON TO THE INSIDE AND SEW ON.

Ⓑ

Ⓐ

SEW THE BOTTOM CLOSED.

Ⓒ

SEW EACH END OF THE STRAP TO THE INSIDE OF THE WAISTLINE.

Lights, Camera . . .

Follow these simple steps to become an amateur film projectionist!

What You'll Need

- clear acetate (available at art-supply stores)
- half-gallon milk carton
- markers, various colors
- scissors
- flashlight
- tape
- ruler

Directions

1. Begin by washing and drying the milk carton thoroughly. Cut off the top and the bottom so that you have a rectangular tube for your "viewer."

2. Next, cut two slits, each about 3" high, on opposite sides of the carton (A).

3. Now cut strips of acetate, each just under 3" wide. Tape them together into one long "filmstrip."

4. Use a marker to divide the acetate strip into a series of frames, each about 3½" wide. Now, leaving the first frame empty, draw scenes on the frames using different-colored markers. The scenes should tell a story.

5. Slide your "filmstrip" through one slit in the carton and out the other so that the first scene is inside the carton.

6. Turn off the lights. Shine the flashlight through an open end of the carton and onto a blank wall (B). The images you drew will be projected onto the wall. Pull the acetate through, frame by frame, until your "movie" is over!

One Step Further

Add color and character to your film projector by covering it with construction paper. Or papier-mâché it and then paint it. Add the name of your favorite movie theater. Make miniature projectors with pint-size cartons or quart-size cartons.

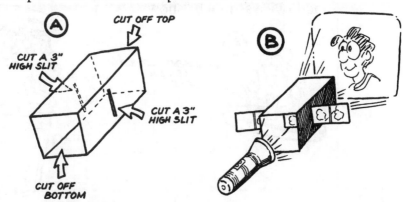

CUT OFF TOP

CUT A 3" HIGH SLIT

CUT A 3" HIGH SLIT

CUT OFF BOTTOM

Shake It Up!

In just a snap, you can make a snazzy snow-dome paperweight like those you see in souvenir shops!

What You'll Need

- empty baby food jar with lid
- small amount of rubber cement
- small plastic flower and stem
- teaspoon
- silver glitter
- water
- glue

Directions

1. First, clean out the baby food jar. Wash the label off.

2. Hold the flower next to the jar. If it's taller than the jar, cut the stem to fit.

3. Next, take the lid and turn it upside down so that the inside part is facing up. Put the lid on the table and put a drop or two of rubber cement in the center of the lid.

4. Attach the flower by sticking its stem in the rubber cement (A). Hold the flower for a few minutes until the rubber cement hardens. If the flower is not secure, add another drop or two of rubber cement and let it dry.

5. Now fill the jar with water until the water is about ¼" from the top. Put 2 teaspoons of the glitter into the water for the "snow."

6. Put glue around the inside edge of the lid, and put a few drops of glue around the rim of the jar, too (B). Screw the lid on. Make sure the jar is upright (the flower will be hanging upside down), and let the glue dry.

7. Turn the jar so the flower is upright. Shake, shake, shake!

One Step Further

Substitute small plastic figures for the plastic flower. Make sure they fit in the jar, though. Put in sequins instead of glitter, or combine the two! Use a jelly jar or other glass jar— then you can use larger plastic figures and add twice as much "snow"!

(A) CEMENT FLOWER TO CENTER OF LID.

APPLY GLUE TO INSIDE OF LID...

...AND TO JAR'S RIM

(B)

28 Carton Critters

The steps below will show you how to make a chick out of an egg carton, but after that, think of some critters to make on your own!

What You'll Need

- cardboard egg carton
- tempera paints, various colors
- buttons, feathers, sequins, colored tissue paper
- paintbrush
- scissors
- glue
- ruler

Directions

1. To make the head, cut off an end pair of cones from the egg carton. On one side of each cone you will see a pointed piece. This is the chick's beak. Hold on to this piece and trim off about ¾" around the edge of the cone. Don't cut off the beak!

2. Fold out the beak on each cone so that it sticks out. Put glue around the edge of one cone. Turn the other cone upside down and press it down on top of the first cone, matching up the beak pieces (A). Let the glue dry, then trim the beak a little.

3. Now it's time to make the chick's body. Cut off another pair of cones (not the other end pair). Each of these cones will have two points sticking up. Hold on to the points of one cone and trim off about ¾" around the edge (don't cut off the points— they're your chick's wings). Take the other cone and do the same, but this time cut off its two points.

4. Fold out the two points on the first cone to make them stick out. Then take the second cone and glue it on top of the other cone (B).

5. Now glue the head onto the body. Let it dry.

6. Paint the chick yellow with an orange beak. Glue on buttons for eyes and feathers for its tail. Add sequins and pieces of tissue paper to make it bright and cheerful!

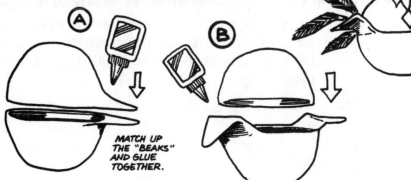

MATCH UP THE "BEAKS" AND GLUE TOGETHER.

Paper Perfect

ADULT SUPERVISION RECOMMENDED
Did you know that you can actually make a sheet of paper right in your own home? Here's how!

What You'll Need

- 30 sheets of regular facial tissue
- baking pan, baking dish, or tub (about 8" x 10" large and 2" deep)
- iron
- large mixing bowl
- liquid measuring cup
- piece of wire window screen, small enough to fit in the pan, dish, or tub
- eggbeater
- liquid laundry starch
- newspaper
- clean rag
- hot water

Directions

1. Before you begin, lay down at least a dozen sheets of newspaper. These will serve as your blotters.

2. First, you'll need to make the pulp. Fill the bowl halfway with hot water (but not too hot to touch). Shred the tissues into small pieces and put them in the water. Put your fingers in the water and shred the tissues further until they dissolve. The pulp will look like thin breakfast cereal.

3. Mix in 2 ounces of starch to help strengthen the paper.

4. Now pour the pulp into the baking pan, dish, or tub. Add enough water to raise the level to at least 1" from the bottom of the pan. Stir vigorously using the eggbeater.

5. Next, slide the screen into the water, then slowly pull it out using both hands. Some of the pulp will be carried out with the screen. Hold the screen over the pan to drain the excess water, and gently shake the screen to distribute the pulp evenly (A).

6. When almost all the water has drained off, lay the screen on the newspapers. Let the pulp dry until it is damp.

7. While the paper is still damp, peel it off the screen. Put a clean rag over the paper and press it with a warm iron (B). This will compress the fibers and strengthen the paper. You should be able to make four to six sheets of paper with each batch of your "paper recipe."

One Step Further

Substitute newspapers or typing paper for the facial tissues. Try adding a few drops of enamel oil paints for color. Take sheets of notebook paper, put them between two sheets of your homemade paper, and bind them together to make a diary or journal!

GENTLY SHAKE SCREEN TO EVENLY DISTRIBUTE THE PULP.

30

This One's for the Birds!

Have fun watching your fine feathered friends by creating these simple but effective bird feeders using ordinary household objects! You can buy birdseed at any grocery or pet supply store.

Directions

Bleach Bottle Feeder

For this feeder, cut four 3" x 3" windows out of the sides of an empty, rinsed bleach bottle. The windows should start 1" from the bottom of the container. Sand down the rough edges with sandpaper or cover the edges with black electrical tape. Next, use a hammer and large nail to poke a hole in the middle of the bottle cap. Cut a 12" piece of string and tie the two ends together. Then thread the looped end through the hole and tie a big knot so the string won't slip through the hole. Now you've got a big loop to hang the bottle feeder from a tree branch or a nail in your roof.

BLEACH BOTTLE FEEDER

PLASTIC BOTTLE FEEDER

Plastic Bottle Feeder

Cut a 3" x 4" window out of an empty 2-liter plastic bottle. The window should be about 2" from the bottom of the bottle. Sand down the edges or tape over them. Now take an empty pie tin and glue it to the bottom of the plastic bottle. To hang up this bird feeder, follow the directions for the Bleach Bottle Feeder.

Mesh Bag Feeder

The mesh bag from fruit or vegetables you buy at some grocery stores makes an ideal bird feeder. You could even use a small mesh laundry bag if you can't find a fruit or vegetable bag. Just fill the empty bag half full with birdseed and tie a knot at the top of the bag. Put string through a hole at the top, tie both ends together, and it's ready to hang!

MESH BAG FEEDER

Pinecone Feeder

Pick up a pinecone or two next time you're walking through your neighborhood or a park. Mix together half a jar of peanut butter, a handful of birdseed, and a handful of uncooked oatmeal in a bowl until the mixture is gooey and sticky. With a butter knife, smear the mixture all over the pinecone. Tie a string around the top for hanging.

SPREAD PEANUT BUTTER-BIRDSEED-OATMEAL MIX ON PINECONE.

PINECONE FEEDER

Doughnut Feeder

You only need a doughnut, two jar lids, some string, and a hammer and nail to make this fun feeder! Use the hammer and nail to make a small hole in the center of each lid. Cut a 12" piece of string. Thread the string through one lid, then through the doughnut hole, then through the other lid. Tie a knot under the bottom lid. Tie the other end of the string onto a tree branch and let it hang (the lids and the doughnut will touch each other). Watch the birds flock to your new feeder!

DOUGHNUT FEEDER

One Step Further

Try making a Nest Helper. Find a pants hanger that has a cardboard tube around the bottom. With a craft knife, cut a row of slats on both sides of the tube. Stuff strands of thread or light string into the slats so that they hang down. Put the hanger on a branch and watch the birds take the thread to build their nests!

PUT STRING THROUGH SLATS.

NEST HELPER

What a Relief!

31

ADULT SUPERVISION REQUIRED
You can have a ball molding homemade dough into a nifty relief map—and learn a little about geography at the same time!

What You'll Need

- 3 cups flour
- 1 cup salt
- 3 tablespoons dry wheat paste powder
- 1¼ cups lukewarm water
- wooden spoon
- 11" x 17" piece of cardboard
- 11"x 17" piece of white construction paper
- large mixing bowl
- craft paints, various colors
- glue
- frying pan
- pencil
- atlas
- paintbrushes

Directions

1. Begin by drawing the shape of the United States on the white construction paper. Use an atlas as a guide. Glue the paper onto the cardboard.

2. You need to make the dough next. Heat the salt in the frying pan over low heat for about five minutes. Then mix the salt, flour, and paste powder together in a bowl. Slowly add the lukewarm water as you continue to stir. If the mixture feels too dry, add water. Knead the dough until it's soft and pliable.

3. Then, still using the atlas as a guide, use chunks of dough to fill in your map! Do the mountain ranges first, starting with the Sierra Nevadas. Make some mountaintops low and ragged, others high and smooth. Fill in the rest of the map with dough, then let it dry.

4. Now paint the details! Put snow and trees on the mountaintops. Paint in all the lakes, rivers, and waterways. Paint each state a different color, and use a smaller brush to add the name of each state.

Soapy Sculptures

ADULT SUPERVISION REQUIRED
Learn how to turn a plain bar of soap into a "squeaky clean" sculpture!

What You'll Need

- bar of soap, any kind
- kitchen knife
- pencil

Directions

1. First, use the pencil to draw the outline of an animal directly on the bar of soap. Take up as much of the bar as you can. Draw a bear, cat, fish, alligator, bird—any animal you'd like. Refer to a photo book of real animals if you need help.
2. Take the knife and carve around the outline you drew, cutting off the excess soap.
3. Now use the knife to carefully shape the animal and make it three-dimensional. Be careful not to cut yourself. You can sprinkle water on the soap to help you mold it more easily. Water also gets rid of any mistakes you may make!
4. Cut small notches to show muscle definition. Try making cross-hatching marks to add texture. For example, if you're carving an alligator, a cross-hatching pattern on its back will make your gator look more real.

One Step Further

For variety, try different-colored soaps. Try making a lizard out of a bar of green soap. Turn a pink cake of soap into a flamingo or white soap into a swan. Or try your hand at sculpting other objects such as seashells or mushrooms. To make your soapy creations more realistic, paint them with craft paints! (If you paint them, just use them for decoration—don't wash your hands with them!)

An Egg-citing Mobile

Colored eggshells are what give this fun mobile an egg-stra special look!

What You'll Need

- 7 raw eggs
- construction paper, any color
- small paintbrushes
- craft paints, various colors
- penny
- pencil
- scissors
- needle and thread
- tissue or crepe paper, various colors
- wire hanger
- cup
- liquid laundry starch
- ruler
- water
- large mixing bowl

Directions

1. Follow the directions under "Walking on Eggshells" (p. 155) to blow out the insides of the eggs. Then cut or tear small strips of the tissue or crepe paper. Papier-mâché the eggshells and the wire hanger with bright colors (see "It's a Piñata!" on p. 19 for directions). You can also paint some of the eggshells with craft paints.

2. Using the pencil, trace the penny on the construction paper and cut it out. Cut a 16" piece of thread, double it up, and thread the needle, tying a big knot at the end of the thread.

3. Now poke the needle through the center of the construction paper circle. Slide the circle all the way down to the knot (A).

4. Choose an eggshell. Push the needle through the smaller hole. Shake the egg gently to make the needle come out the larger hole. Grab the needle and slide the eggshell down to the paper circle (A). Cut off the thread and tie it onto the bottom of the hanger so that the egg hangs down.

5. Repeat Steps 2 through 4 for the remaining eggs, except cut alternating long and short pieces of thread so the eggs hang at varying lengths (B).

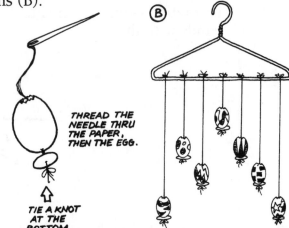

Ⓐ

THREAD THE NEEDLE THRU THE PAPER, THEN THE EGG.

TIE A KNOT AT THE BOTTOM.

Ⓑ

 # Melted Plastic Ornaments

ADULT SUPERVISION REQUIRED
Here's a way to make cool ornaments right in your own kitchen!

What You'll Need

- plastic berry baskets
- small glass beads
- plastic-coated wire (available at hardware stores)
- 3- or 4-quart saucepan
- aluminum pie pan
- water
- kitchen tongs
- scissors
- glue
- glitter
- ruler

Directions

1. Fill the saucepan with water and heat it on the stove (but don't boil it). The water should be deep enough to completely cover the basket.

2. Drop a plastic basket into the hot water. When the basket has collapsed and changed shape, pull it out using the tongs. Put it on a pie pan to cool.

3. Now string some glass beads onto a 24" piece of coated wire. Make sure to cut off any wire ends that are showing. Weave the beads in and out of the holes in the basket. The wire will conform to the shape of the basket.

4. Put dabs of glue on various areas of the basket and sprinkle glitter over it.

5. To make a hanger, cut another piece of coated wire about 5" long. Weave it through one of the holes. Tie both ends together at the top.

One Step Further

Try dropping a plastic cup into the hot water. It will melt into a nifty bell shape. Use colored cups for variety. To make a hole for hanging, ask an adult to heat the point of a large sewing needle by holding a lit match to it for a few seconds. Then poke a hole in the plastic with the heated needle.

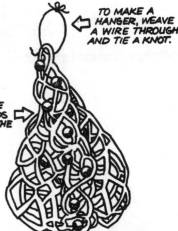

TO MAKE A HANGER, WEAVE A WIRE THROUGH AND TIE A KNOT.

WEAVE THE WIRED BEADS THROUGH THE BASKET.

Balloon Blastoff!

Learn how to make a nifty balloon rocket that actually takes off! You'll need a friend to help you with this one.

What You'll Need

- fishing line
- plastic drinking straw
- balloon
- masking tape

Directions

1. Start by measuring out a piece of fishing line the length of your bedroom or living room.
2. Tie one end to a doorknob or a piece of heavy furniture at one end of the room.
3. Next, run the fishing line through a straw. Then stretch the line across the room and attach the other end to another doorknob or piece of furniture.
4. Blow up the balloon and pinch the end to hold in the air. Have your friend tape the top of the balloon to the straw so that the balloon hangs down.
5. Still holding the balloon closed, walk the straw and balloon to one end of the fishing line. Turn so that you are facing the opposite end of the fishing line.
6. Now start your countdown! When you reach zero, let go of the balloon. The escaping air will act as jet propulsion to push the balloon forward on the fishing line!

One Step Further

You can string more than one fishing line across the room and have a balloon-rocket race with your friends. Or you can use this method as an intercom to send secret messages to your brother or sister in another room. Just tape a note to the balloon and let 'er rip! Experiment a little. Get an adult to help you string fishing line from the roof or a tree so your blastoff can be vertical!

 **Cotton Swab Art**

Create a nifty double-sided piece of art using simple cotton swabs!

What You'll Need

- 3 to 4 large boxes of cotton swabs (those with wooden sticks work best)
- color markers
- craft paints, various colors
- narrow paintbrush
- light cardboard
- scissors
- tape
- ruler

- 2 pieces of plastic canvas, about 6½" x 6½" with 5 holes per inch (available in the needlepoint section at craft stores)

Directions

1. To start, push a cotton swab through a square in one piece of the plastic canvas. You're going to fill the whole canvas using the swabs.

2. Now line up the second piece of canvas with the first one. Push the swab through the second piece to "connect" the canvases.

3. Take another swab and poke it through each canvas next to the first swab. Continue doing this, filling up each row (A). When you're through, the two pieces of canvas should stand upright on their own.

4. Now turn one side of the canvas toward you. Think of an outdoor scene, a mosaic, whatever you like. Then start painting the tips of the swabs (B). Be careful not to make a mistake (it will be difficult to replace the swabs). When you're done, paint a different scene or design on the other side.

5. To make the frame, measure the space between the two pieces of canvas. Cut a strip of cardboard so that it is a little wider than that space. The strip should be long enough to wrap all the way around your artwork.

6. Color the frame using the paints or markers. Then wrap it around your cotton swab art and tape it at the bottom (B). Your masterpiece is done!

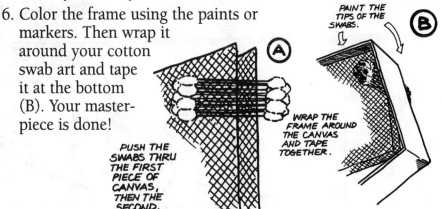

PUSH THE SWABS THRU THE FIRST PIECE OF CANVAS, THEN THE SECOND.

PAINT THE TIPS OF THE SWABS.

WRAP THE FRAME AROUND THE CANVAS AND TAPE TOGETHER.

37 A Really Big Shoe

Take a "step" in the right direction by turning an old shoe into a playful planter!

What You'll Need

- big, old shoe (canvas works best, but leather is fine, too)
- small indoor or outdoor plant (such as a cactus or African violet) that fits inside the shoe
- liquid laundry starch
- newspaper
- paintbrush
- tempera paints, various colors
- water
- cup

Directions

1. Before you begin, lay some sheets of newspaper on your work table.

2. Now put the shoe on the newspaper. If there are any shoelaces, remove them. Papier-mâché the entire shoe, following the instructions given in "It's a Pinata!" (p. 101). Do two layers of papier-mâché, allowing the first layer to dry before you apply the next.

3. Once the shoe is stiff and dry, paint it! Be creative. Make lightning bolts, symbols, or fake buckles and laces. Let the paint dry overnight.

4. Now, leaving the plant in its original pot, place it inside the shoe. Try this nifty craft again using a different kind of shoe—maybe a high-top or a penny loafer!

38

A Rose Is a Rose

Even a paper rose by any other name is still a beautiful rose.

What You'll Need

- red and green tissue paper
- cup or bowl
- scissors

- wire stems and florist's tape (available at florist's shops)

- glass bottle
- pencil
- stapler
- ruler

Directions

1. First, cut 18 squares of red tissue paper. Each square should be 4" x 4".

2. Next, put the cup or bowl upside down on a stack of about four tissues and trace around it with the pencil. Cut out the circles. Repeat until you have 18 circles.

3. Then make a small loop at one end of a wire stem. Thread six circles onto the stem by poking the pointed end through the center of each circle. Bunch the circles loosely around the loop, then staple them once at the bottom (A).

4. Do the same with six more circles and staple them onto the others. Then repeat with the last six circles.

5. Now cut a long piece of florist's tape. With one hand, hold one end of the tape over the last staple. Use your other hand to wrap tape around the bottom of the flower about three or four times. Then continue winding tape down and around the stem.

6. Don't forget the leaves! Cut four 4" x 4" squares out of the green tissue paper. Now stack them and cut out a three-leaf shape. Tape the leaves onto the wire (B).

7. Finally, fluff out the rose layer by layer so it looks like it's in bloom. You can put it into a small glass bottle that's been decorated with papier-mâché or paints and give it as a gift!

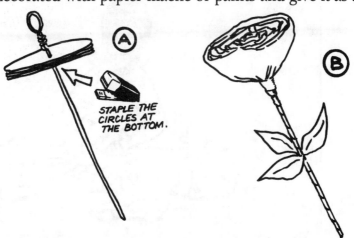

STAPLE THE CIRCLES AT THE BOTTOM.

 **Rolling in Dough**

ADULT SUPERVISION RECOMMENDED
You'll be amazed at all the things you can do with this homemade dough. Just follow the simple recipe below.

What You'll Need

- 4 cups flour
- 1 cup salt
- 1½ cups water
- large mixing bowl
- newspaper
- nonstick (or greased) disposable cookie sheet
- craft paints, various colors
- wooden spoon
- paintbrush
- spray lacquer
- oven mitts

Directions

1. In the mixing bowl, combine the flour, salt, and water and mix well with the wooden spoon.
2. Mold the dough into different shapes, such as fruits, vegetables, animals, creepy insects, or miniature animals. Spread them out on the cookie sheet and bake at 350 degrees for one hour.
3. Use oven mitts to take out the dough and let it cool. Then paint the shapes.
4. When the paint is dry, take the figures outside and place them on sheets of newspaper. Spray them with lacquer to keep the paint from chipping.

One Step Further

You can make all sorts of crafts with this moldable dough. Glue a magnet on the back of your creation and stick it on the refrigerator. Make Christmas or Hanukkah ornaments. Just glue a piece of thread or string on the back of the ornament and it's ready to hang! You can also roll beads of different shapes, poke a nail through each to make a hole, and bake the beads. Then paint them, string them, and make necklaces and bracelets!

Make a Good Impression

Did you know that you can create interesting textures and patterns using simple household objects—including fruits and vegetables?

What You'll Need

- tempera paints, various colors
- apples, potatoes, starfruit
- stack of continuous feed computer paper
- several sponges
- empty spools, clothespins, buttons, corks, bottle caps
- 2 wooden dowels, at least 1" wider than the computer paper
- glue
- scissors
- string
- kitchen knife
- several empty milk cartons
- ruler

Directions

1. First, prepare your printing tools. Slice a raw potato in half and carve a heart on the inside of one half. Then dig out the potato around the heart so that the heart sticks up. Leave the other half uncut. Do the same with the apple, except cut a different shape. Cut the starfruit in half. Cut some of the sponges into squares, circles, and triangles.

2. To make a stamp pad, cut a clean milk carton to about 3" high. Cut a sponge to fit, moisten it with water, and pour some paint on it. Do the same with another milk carton and a different color of paint.

3. Spread out several sheets of computer paper, but don't tear them apart.

4. Now go stamp crazy! Choose a printing tool, such as one mentioned above, dip it in your stamp pad, and stamp it all over the paper (A). Repeat with a different tool and a different color. Be sure to leave the paper blank at the top and bottom to roll around the dowel.

5. When you're finished, tear your artwork off at the top and bottom and let it dry. Then put glue on a wooden dowel and roll the top sheet around it twice. Take the second dowel and do the same with the bottom sheet.

6. Cut a piece of string about 2' long. Tie each end to opposite ends of the top dowel. Now your artwork is ready to hang (B)!

As Time Goes By

Dig out those mementos of yours and turn them into a great gift your mom or dad will treasure forever!

What You'll Need

- large piece of cardboard, at least 16" by 20"
- crayons, markers, and paints (various colors)
- paintbrush
- scissors
- glue
- award ribbons, certificates, report cards, tests, book reports, baby photos, your horoscope, your baby bracelet, school assembly programs, pictures you drew, a lock of your hair, and other mementos

Directions

1. Make sure you have permission from an adult to use all the mementos you've chosen for this project. Gather all your mementos in front of you. Take some of the bigger items—such as newspaper clippings and pictures you drew—and trim them into different shapes.

2. Start gluing the items on the cardboard one by one. You might want to arrange them loosely in some sort of design first, then glue them down. Or just put them down in a random pattern. Overlap the items so no cardboard shows through.

3. Now add artistic flair to your collage by swashing strokes of paint here and there, outlining some of the items in crayon, and underlining important things in marker.

4. Once your collage is finished, ask an adult to help you get it framed. You can buy the supplies to make a frame at an art store, or have the art store frame the picture for you. This collage makes a wonderful gift for your mom or dad. After all, you wouldn't be here if it weren't for them!

Rockin' Candy

ADULT SUPERVISION REQUIRED
In one week, you can grow your own rock candy mountain. See if you can wait that long to eat it!

What You'll Need

- 1 cup water
- 4 cups sugar
- piece of heavy cord (the length of the jar)
- 3- or 4-quart saucepan
- large glass jar
- oven mitts
- wooden spoon
- dinner plate
- pencil

Directions

1. To begin, put the water and 2 cups of the sugar into the saucepan and heat over the stove, stirring with the wooden spoon until the sugar has dissolved.

2. Stir in the remaining 2 cups of sugar little by little. Continue heating until all the sugar has dissolved. Then have an adult help you pour all the liquid into the glass jar, using oven mitts.

3. Now tie one end of the cord around the middle of the pencil. Balance the pencil over the mouth of the jar so that the cord hangs down into the liquid. In a few hours, sugar crystals will begin to form on the cord.

4. The next day, take out the cord and place it on a dinner plate. You'll notice that crystals have also formed on the sides of the jar. To get rid of these, pour the liquid out of the jar into the saucepan and reheat it.

5. When the liquid is hot (but not boiling), have an adult help you pour it back into the jar, using oven mitts. The liquid will dissolve the crystals on the sides of the jar. Let the liquid cool.

6. When the liquid is lukewarm, put the cord with the crystals back into the jar, resting the pencil over the mouth.

7. Repeat Steps 4 through 6 every day for a week until you have a big rock candy mountain!

Paper Sculpture

ADULT SUPERVISION REQUIRED

Don't get this challenging craft confused with papier-mâché. Paper sculpture involves bending, scoring, and folding flat paper to make three-dimensional art! The steps below will show you how to make a paper-sculpture poodle.

What You'll Need

- heavy paper, such as drawing paper or construction paper
- craft knife or single-edged razor blade
- rubber cement or glue
- newspapers or thick cardboard
- notebook paper or typing paper
- ruler
- pencil
- scissors

Directions

1. Start with a sheet of heavy paper that is at least 12" x 8". Lay the paper horizontally. Put a stack of newspapers or a piece of thick cardboard underneath to protect your work surface.

2. With the pencil, draw a side view of a dog. You only need to draw one front leg and one back leg, but make them wide, because you will be scoring and bending them to look like four legs (A). Try to use up most of the paper. Then cut out the dog.

3. To score his legs, lightly draw a slightly curved line to divide the front leg into two legs. Do the same to the back leg. Then carefully run, or score, the back of the hobby knife or razor blade along the lines you drew (B). Press just hard enough to score the top layer of the paper. Don't cut right through the paper.

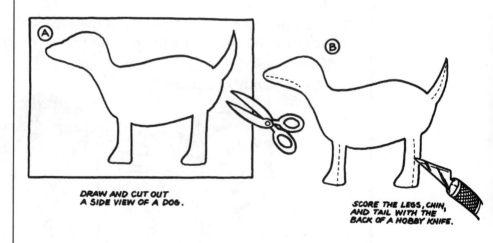

DRAW AND CUT OUT
A SIDE VIEW OF A DOG.

SCORE THE LEGS, CHIN,
AND TAIL WITH THE
BACK OF A HOBBY KNIFE.

4. Now gently fold the legs along the cuts you made so that the lines you scored stick up and are outside the fold, facing you (C). Score the tail and chin the same way.

5. Next, you'll need to make fringes for your poodle's head, body, legs, and tail. Cut several strips of the notebook paper or typing paper. Each strip should be at least 2" wide. Vary the length depending on the size of the head, the tail, and so forth. Cut slits in each strip, then curl them by running them over the sharp edge of a scissors blade or a ruler (D).

6. Now attach each fringe of curls to your poodle using rubber cement or glue. Put each fringe right up against the other to create rows of curls. You can mount your paper sculpture by rubber-cementing it to a construction paper background of a contrasting color to make your art stand out (E).

One Step Further

You can create all sorts of things with paper sculpture—just put your mind to it! Use different-colored paper for variety. Cut semi-circles and bend them out to make eyes, mouths, and other features. Once you know how to score the paper, you can create all sorts of three-dimensional effects. Just remember that the scored lines are always on the outside of the folds, so try scoring both sides of the paper and bending it both ways for that "3-D" look!

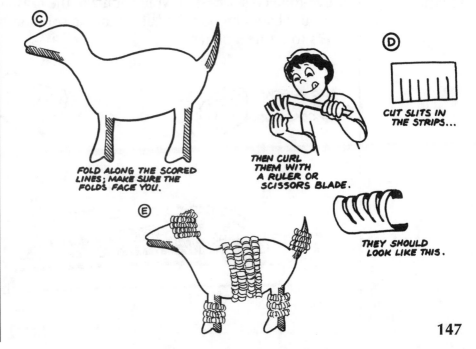

Ⓒ FOLD ALONG THE SCORED LINES; MAKE SURE THE FOLDS FACE YOU.

THEN CURL THEM WITH A RULER OR SCISSORS BLADE.

Ⓓ CUT SLITS IN THE STRIPS...

THEY SHOULD LOOK LIKE THIS.

Ⓔ

Magic Crystals

Use ordinary charcoal to grow colorful crystals right before your eyes!

What You'll Need

- charcoal briquettes
- disposable shallow cooking pan
- food coloring, any color
- paper cup
- mixing spoon

- 3 tablespoons salt
- 3 tablespoons liquid bluing (available at grocery stores)
- 3 tablespoons clear ammonia

Directions

1. Begin by spreading out enough charcoal briquettes to cover the bottom of the cooking pan.

2. Put a few drops of food coloring over the briquettes.

3. Mix the salt, bluing, and ammonia together in the paper cup and pour the solution over the charcoal. Be careful not to smell the ammonia directly. In just a few hours, crystals will start to grow!

4. You need to coat the charcoal with the solution each day. Just repeat Step 3. When you think they've grown enough, stop applying the liquid.

One Step Further

Try using different colors of food coloring to create two-tone or three-tone crystals. See if you can make the crystals grow into various shapes by pouring the ammonia solution over certain areas to create a pattern.

ADD A FEW DROPS OF FOOD COLORING.

THEN ADD THE AMMONIA MIXTURE.

45 Bull-Roarer

ADULT SUPERVISION REQUIRED

According to folklore, when the Native Americans whirled bull-roarers over their heads, the whooshing sound resembled the wind blowing. The Native Americans used bull-roarers to summon rain.

What You'll Need

- thin, flat piece of wood at least 6" long
- ruler
- sandpaper or a heavy file
- cord or string
- drill
- scissors

Directions

1. Get an adult to help you make the bull-roarer. The piece of wood can be any rectangular or square shape, just as long as it's thin and flat. Taper two opposing sides using the file or sandpaper. Then file down one end to create a rounded shape. File it down until it's smooth.

2. Next, drill a hole in the opposite end near the edge. Cut a piece of cord or string, 3' to 4' long. Put one end through the hole and tie a tight knot.

3. Now test your bull-roarer! It's best not to do this in the house. Go outside and stand in an area where you won't hit anything or anyone. Whirl the bull-roarer over your head in a fast circular motion. Don't be surprised if the sound comes and goes; that's how the bull-roarer works.

One Step Further

You can paint bright colors and patterns on your bull-roarer. Try making a bull-roarer using an oval or circular piece of wood this time. Try different sizes of wood, too. See if there's any difference in the sound each one makes.

WHRRRRR!

FILE DOWN SIDES AND ROUND OFF THE TOP.

I Spy Tie-Dye

ADULT SUPERVISION REQUIRED

The art of tie-dyeing is so simple and fun, no wonder it's still as popular today as it was during the sixties!

What You'll Need

- empty 1-gallon bottle
- old clothes, such as T-shirts or shorts
- 3 plastic buckets or large bowls
- rubber gloves or clothespin
- bleach
- apron or smock
- string or rubber bands
- newspaper
- dye (Rit® or Tintex®), various colors
- old towels
- water

Directions

1. For light-colored fabric, use dye. For dark-colored fabric, use bleach. Put on the apron or smock before you start. To prepare the dye: Pour a package of dye powder, any color, into the gallon bottle and fill it with hot tap water. Put the top on and shake well. Pour the liquid into a plastic bucket or bowl. To prepare the bleach: Pour the bleach about 2" deep into another plastic bucket or bowl. Do this outside or near an open window. Don't touch the bleach or smell it directly! Fill the third bucket or bowl with plain water.

2. Now tie string or rubber bands around the fabric in as many places as you want (A).

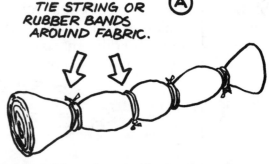

TIE STRING OR RUBBER BANDS AROUND FABRIC. (A)

3. It is best to always wear rubber gloves when you're dipping fabric. If you don't have gloves, use a clothespin to pick up the fabric. Dip the fabric into the dye or bleach for two to three minutes (B). You can put the whole piece of fabric in, or just dip the parts that are tied. For light-colored fabrics, wait until the fabric is a little darker than you want it to be. For dark-colored fabrics, wait until it has turned as light as you want it to be.

4. Pick up the fabric and dip it into the bucket or bowl of plain water, then remove it and let it drip.

5. Wrap the fabric in some old towels and press down on it to soak up the water.

6. Take off the string or rubber bands and hang up the fabric to dry. Put newspapers below to catch any dripping water. You'll have a great piece of tie-dye overnight!

One Step Further

You can tie-dye the same shirt or piece of clothing in different colors. Get an extra bucket or bowl for each color. After the first dipping, rinse the fabric but don't remove the string or rubber bands. Then dip the fabric into a different-colored dye. Change the rinse water after each color. Try tie-dyeing old pillowcases or bedsheets!

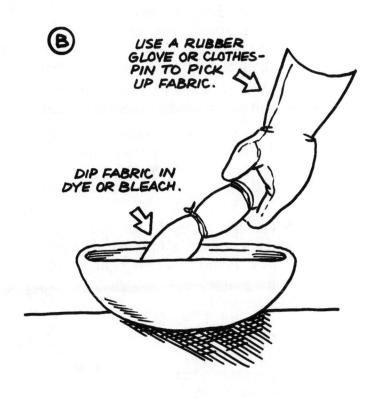

Ⓑ USE A RUBBER GLOVE OR CLOTHES-PIN TO PICK UP FABRIC.

DIP FABRIC IN DYE OR BLEACH.

Dancing Marionettes

Everybody loves puppets. Here's how to make your very own marionette!

What You'll Need

- lightweight cardboard, 8½" x 11"
- yarn, any color
- tempera paints or markers (various colors)
- 12" wooden stick
- scissors
- brass fasteners or rivets
- paintbrush
- hole punch
- heavy thread
- pencil
- glue
- ruler

Directions

1. Start by using the pencil to draw a person on the cardboard. Make sure the arms and legs are wide enough. Use the paint or markers to fill in the face and clothing.

2. Now cut the person out of the cardboard. To make hair, cut some short strands of yarn and glue them on top of the head.

3. Get ready to perform "surgery"! Cut off the feet, then cut again at the knees, then cut the legs off at the hips. Now cut off the hands, then cut at the elbows, then cut the arms off at the shoulders. All that's left should be the head and torso.

4. Next, punch holes in the arms and legs with the hole punch and use the brass fasteners to reattach each limb (A).

5. Now make the marionette's strings. Cut six 4" pieces of thread. Then cut six 9" pieces of thread. Tie the ends of the 4" pieces to the fasteners at the back of your marionette's wrists, elbows, and shoulders. Next, tie the longer pieces to the fasteners at the hips, knees, and feet.

6. One by one, tie the free ends to the wooden stick, spreading them out across the stick. The threads on the marionette's right side should be on the right half of the stick, and the threads on the puppet's left side should be on the left half. Rock the stick back and forth and watch your merry marionette dance (B)!

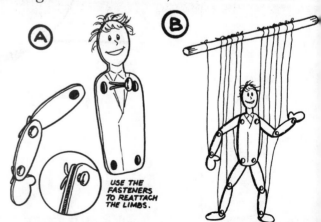

USE THE FASTENERS TO REATTACH THE LIMBS.

Lionhearted!

Instead of throwing out old washcloths, save them to make a little washcloth lion face!

What You'll Need

- 2 old washcloths
- fabric scraps, old socks, yarn, foam rubber, cotton balls
- tape from an old audiocassette
- sewing machine (or needle and thread)
- buttons
- scissors
- felt
- fabric glue (available at craft stores)
- ruler

Directions

1. Start by making the lion's face on one of the washcloths. Sew on buttons for the lion's eyes. Cut pieces of felt for the ears, nose, whiskers, and mouth and glue them on.

2. To make the lion's mane, pull out the tape from an audiocassette. Cut the tape into 4"-long strips. Then lay down the second washcloth and glue the strips along the four sides of it so that they hang out over the sides (A). Overlap some of them to add thickness to the mane.

3. After the glue has dried, put any combination of fabric scraps, cutup socks, yarn, pieces of foam rubber, and cotton balls on top of the second washcloth. A handful or two should be enough.

4. Now place the first washcloth over the second one to cover the stuffing. Sew the washcloths together along all four sides, using small, tight stitches (A).

One Step Further

Try making a girl's or boy's face. Add human facial features using felt and buttons. Use cassette tape or colored yarn on the top side for hair.

LET STRIPS HANG OUT OVER EDGE.

THEN SEW ALL SIDES SHUT.

A Dandy Desk Set

If this "leather" desk set were real, it would probably cost $200, but you can make it for just pennies!

What You'll Need

- small glass bottle
- empty frozen juice can
- 12" x 18" piece of cardboard
- cigar box
- two 12" x 18" pieces of construction paper, any color
- empty baby food jar
- masking tape
- brown shoe polish
- newspaper
- ruler
- glue

Directions

1. First, lay down sheets of newspaper to cover your work surface. Clean and dry the frozen juice can. Tear off pieces of masking tape to cover the outside of the can completely.

2. Now rub shoe polish over the tape until all the pieces are colored brown. Once the polish is dry, you've got a pencil holder!

3. Repeat Steps 1 and 2, this time turning the baby food jar into a paper clip holder! Next, make the glass bottle into a flower vase or a letter-opener holder. Cover a cigar box with tape and polish and use it as a letter holder.

4. Now it's time to create a desk blotter. Take a sheet of the construction paper and cut out four right triangles with 3" bases (A). These will be the four corners of the blotter.

5. Cover the triangles with short strips of masking tape, then rub shoe polish over them. Lay a triangle on each corner of the piece of cardboard so that the right angles line up.

6. Next, carefully glue only the right edges of the triangles onto the cardboard. The edges that face toward the middle of the blotter should not be glued down. Insert the second piece of construction paper into your blotter, tucking a corner under each triangle (B).

(A)

3" BASE
CUT OUT FOUR RIGHT TRIANGLES WITH 3" BASES.

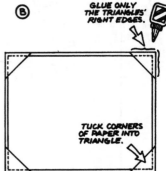

(B)

GLUE ONLY THE TRIANGLES' RIGHT EDGES.

TUCK CORNERS OF PAPER INTO TRIANGLE.

Walking on Eggshells

Did you know you can dress up bottles, boxes, and cans with crushed eggshells? It's eggs-traordinary!

What You'll Need

- 12 raw eggs
- large mixing bowl
- glass bottle, shoe box, or tin can
- needle
- newspaper
- tempera paints, various colors
- glue
- paintbrush

Directions

1. Blow out the insides of the eggs first. Hold an egg over the mixing bowl. Make a hole in one end of the egg with the needle. Then make a hole in the other end, but don't take the needle out. Move the needle around inside the egg until the hole is about ½" wide. Remove the needle. Blow through the smaller hole. The inside of the egg will come out of the bigger hole. Rinse out the egg with cool water and repeat with the remaining eggs. (Don't throw the insides away—cook them for breakfast!)

2. Spread out a few sheets of newspaper and put the empty shells on top. Cover them with another sheet of newspaper. Now get your shoes on and stomp all over the shells to crush them. When you're through, take off the top sheet of newspaper.

3. Put glue all over the bottle, shoe box, or can. Then roll it in the crushed eggshells, making sure it gets completely covered. Let the glue dry.

4. Finally, use the tempera paints to paint the eggshells. Make stripes, polka dots, zigzag patterns . . . use your imagination!

Hosting a Craft Fair

Is everyone raving about the crafts you're making? Are you having so much fun that you don't want to stop? Well, have you ever thought about hosting a craft fair?

A craft fair is a great way to make some money. You can do it as a fund-raiser for a local charity or to get money for a neighborhood project. You can organize a craft fair to raise money for your school's student council. You can even hold a craft fair to make some money to buy a new bicycle.

Hosting a craft fair should be fun, but it requires a bit of thought and energy. Are you ready for a challenge? If you are, you can start preparing right now!

Four to eight weeks before the craft fair

The very first step is to get your parents' permission to host a craft fair. Assure them that you will be responsible for planning the whole event. You may have to borrow supplies or ask for assistance on occasion. It's a good idea to have an adult nearby during your craft fair in case you run into any problems.

Next, consider asking some friends to join you in hosting the craft fair. Invite friends who are responsible and reliable and, most importantly, will also enjoy making crafts. It will be easier and more fun to make crafts, distribute flyers, and organize the craft fair if you are working with friends. If you decide to host a craft fair on your own, try to keep it small. You don't need to do too much—a few nice crafts might be enough.

If you would like to hold a craft fair for a particular cause, present your idea to the other people involved. Prepare as much as possible beforehand so that you'll be ready to answer questions. Offer some ideas for crafts you can sell. Try to figure out how much work this craft fair will entail. Explain why a craft fair would be a great way to raise money for the cause. Be sure to encourage others to share their ideas for the craft fair.

There are many different crafts in this section that you could make for your craft fair. Keep in mind which ones will be easiest to make and which ones might sell well. See pages 160–161 for some ideas. Once you decide which crafts to sell, figure out how many of each craft you will need to make. For example, you could make about six mini-piñatas, rather than one big piñata. Start making crafts as soon as you've set your list. Store them in a safe spot until the craft fair.

Do you want to have a theme for your craft fair? You can try a summer theme or a holiday theme. You can also give your craft fair a creative name to make it more fun. Brainstorm with your friends or look through magazines and newspapers for interesting names or themes.

Choose the location for your craft fair. If you're raising money for a particular cause, you may be able to have the sale at school. Ask a teacher to help you find out what the rules are. If not, choose someone's home. Have it outside (as long as the weather is nice) if you want to catch customers who are just driving by. Ask an adult to check on any neighborhood or city regulations against holding a yard sale. If you are having it inside, consider making the craft fair invitation-only so it's not too crowded.

Decide on a date for your craft fair. It's important to consider how long it will take you to make all the crafts you want to sell. Give yourself plenty of time to work on them after school and on the weekends. When you've come up with a reasonable amount of time, tack on an extra week just in case you run into problems. Ask adults who will be involved what time will be convenient for them. Make sure you select a time when your customers will be able to come. If you're having your craft fair at home, a Saturday or Sunday might be most convenient. If you're selling crafts at school, after the last class or during lunchtime may work the best.

Pick a starting time and an ending time. Make sure you allow yourself plenty of time to set everything up and clean up afterward. A few hours should be plenty of time for your craft fair, unless you have a lot of people who can take turns selling. You'll need to schedule in breaks if you're selling all day!

Two to three weeks before the craft fair

Now invite your friends and family. You can make invitations if you're only giving them to a few people. If you want to attract a lot of customers, you can make flyers and hand them out to people in your community. The invitations or flyers should include the following information:

- who is hosting the craft fair
- what you will be selling—list a few of your favorite crafts
- when it will be—what time it will begin and end, and the date
- where it will be—include directions if necessary
- why you're hosting the craft fair—but only if it's for a cause you think people would be interested in

If you have decided on an invitation-only craft fair, you might want to ask people to RSVP. Include your name and phone number on the invitations so that it will be easy for them to contact you. If you are passing out flyers, make sure that you get a parent's permission first. *Do not put your phone number on flyers that you will be handing out to strangers.*

If your craft fair has a theme or a unique name, be sure to include this on the invitations or flyers. Try to make them fun and creative! Think about how many you will need to make. If it's a lot, consider photocopying them, but plan carefully so that you don't waste money.

As the date of the craft fair nears, keep making crafts. If you're running into problems with any of the crafts, you still have time to choose new ones.

The week before the craft fair

Are all the crafts ready? Add any finishing touches and check over your work.

A few days before the craft fair, decide how much to charge for each craft. Keep track of how much each item cost to make, then add on a bit, or double the amount, to get the price. When you've done that, ask yourself if people will be willing to pay that much. For example, figure out how much it will cost you to make "Works Like a Charm!" on page 95. Is $1.00 too much to charge for it? You and the other craft fair organizers should also decide ahead of time whether or not you will be willing to accept bargaining. A customer may offer to pay you less than what's on the price tag. Will you accept that?

Mark each item's price on a tag. You can use removable stickers, index cards, or signs to display the prices. Make sure the price tags don't damage the crafts. Write the price clearly.

You will need a cash box and some money to make change for your customers. If you don't have a cash box, you can use a shoe box. A calculator may also come in handy. Be sure that you have a pad of paper and a few pencils. Write down each craft item and its price when you sell it. This will help you keep track of which items are selling quickly and how much they have sold for, so that you'll have an idea of what to make for your next craft fair.

Now think of what other materials you will need for the day of the fair. You may need to buy some items. These items cut into your profits, so try to borrow them whenever possible. Ask your parents to save paper bags and boxes for you to use. Try to arrange the crafts on tables with tablecloths if possible. If you don't have tables, you can turn over boxes, cover them with fabric, and place the crafts on top. Presentation is very important, so try to make things look nice.

Give yourself enough time to set everything up before the craft fair begins. Take some time to decorate the area. You can tie a few balloons to the tables or arrange some artificial flowers. Do you have a theme that would be fun to decorate with? Put up signs to grab people's attention, but make sure you have permission first.

The day of the craft fair

Concentrate on having fun! All the hard work you did ahead of time should pay off. Be friendly to your customers. Make yourself available to answer questions.

When it's all done, don't forget to clean up thoroughly, and thank everyone who has helped you.

Whether you're having your craft fair after school or on the weekend, you can bet that you'll work up an appetite! Keep some fruit and crackers on hand for a snack. Or if you think you'll be really hungry, pack a cooler with sandwiches. Also, be sure to have a supply of water nearby.

The Perfect Craft

Although you should be able to make the crafts in this section using items normally found around your home, you may want to buy some materials. If you decide to do that, keep in mind that it will cut into your profits. There are many ways to make the crafts especially appealing—here are a few items that could be best-sellers at a craft fair.

It's a Piñata! (page 101)

Create a bunch of mini-piñatas using small balloons. Sell them with wrapped candies and small toys stuffed inside. With this item, it's a good idea to keep track of what's inside each piñata so that customers can know what they're buying.

Marvelous Marbleized Stationery (page 102)

Create a pencil and paper set your customers will love! Follow the steps described for the craft to make a matching pencil. Attach a clothespin to the eraser, then dip a pencil in the oil paint. Stick the sharpened end of the pencil into a piece of Styrofoam to keep it steady and let it dry overnight.

Candle, Candle, Burning Bright (page 116)

When you're ready to pour the wax into the cartons, ask an adult to carefully drop in rose petals, leaves, and small twigs, or line the milk or juice cartons with these items before you pour in the wax. When the candle is set, wrap a pretty ribbon around the middle of the candle and tie it into a bow.

Paper Perfect (page 130)

Add dried flower petals, leaves, and tiny twigs to the pulp to make some really pretty paper. When the paper is ready, you can stack a few sheets together, tie a ribbon around them, and add a dried flower to finish off the set.

I Spy Tie-Dye (page 150)

Create cool T-shirt and sock sets, or make tie-dyed hair bands. Find clothing items that are made of cotton and are white and washable. Follow the directions with this craft to make different pieces.

Does your craft fair have a theme? If it does, then select some crafts that could follow the theme. Try to think of simple ways you could adapt them. Here's how to make a few crafts for a beach-theme craft fair.

Works Like a Charm! (page 95)

Spread glue over the wooden frame, then cover it with shells and sprinkle on colored sand. After it dries, take it outside, place it on newspaper, and spray it with shellac.

Sublime Chimes (page 96)

This craft would look great with a beach theme! Glue rope around the edges of the cardboard. Cover the cardboard and rope with gold spray paint. After it dries, glue some seashells to the cardboard. Then place additional seashells on string (or glue them to the string) and hang them from the cardboard to catch the wind.

Soapy Sculptures (page 135)

Shape soap into seashells, starfish, or sea lions. You can create a number of fun beach or sea items.

Did your little brother help you set up tables? Did your mom save the day when it started to rain? When the craft fair is over and you've cleaned everything up, there's only one thing left to do. It's time to say thank you to everyone who has helped you out. Make each person's gift unique. With a little extra thought, a set of "Rolling Coasters" or "Sublime Chimes" can make a wonderful gift. If you can, make your thank-you gifts before the craft fair. Otherwise, make them as soon as possible. You should give the gifts to everyone within one week of the craft fair.

Craft Fair Checkoff List

Create your own checkoff list with all the things you'll need to keep track of for your craft fair. You can do it on a computer or by hand. Be sure to include all the important information, as shown on the example below. You can also include flyers/invitations, price tags, signs, and thank-you gifts on your list.

Specifics

Theme: _____

Date: _____

Time: _____ to _____

Place: _____

Other crafters   Phone numbers

_____   _____

_____   _____

Decorations

Need to make   Need to buy

_____   _____

_____   _____

_____   _____

Supplies

Supplies	Number	Who will bring it/buy it
Tables	_____	_____
Chairs	_____	_____
Pencils	_____	_____
Pads of paper	_____	_____
Calculator	_____	_____
Cash box	_____	_____
_____	_____	_____
_____	_____	_____
_____	_____	_____
_____	_____	_____

Crafts

Craft: _____ Done _____

Number	Materials	Who will bring it/buy it
_____	_____	_____
_____	_____	_____
_____	_____	_____
_____	_____	_____

Origami Crafts

NOTE: The numbered pinwheel in the upper right-hand corner of each craft indicates the level of difficulty, 1 being the easiest, 3 being the hardest.

Contents

Introduction

The beautiful, sophisticated origami masterpieces made in Japan at least 1,200 years ago were generally made for ceremonies, festivals, or symbolic purposes. It's not known whether Japanese, Chinese, or Korean people first practiced this creative art form, but the word *origami* comes from the Japanese words *ori* (to fold) and *kami* (paper).

Some of the traditional designs for animals, birds, insects, and objects—first created centuries ago—have never changed. So when you build your origami crafts, you are re-creating history!

There are as many styles and designs of origami and reasons for making it as there are people who create the pieces. Some people love to come up with new ideas and figure out a way to make their designs work. Others enjoy the challenge of taking a diagram in a book and making it into an even better object than what is pictured.

Regardless of which way you prefer to work, origami is inexpensive and a wonderful form of art you can do practically anywhere.

To bring out the best in every origami craft you create and fold, follow these important tips:

- Always work on a clean, hard surface.

- Neatness is most important when it comes to making origami figures. Until you become familiar with the various folds, practice your folding techniques on scratch pieces of paper, trimmed to make all four sides equal.

- Crease firmly and precisely, making each fold even and crisp. The sharper your creases, the better your finished piece will look.

- Never skip a step.

- The best way to become really good at doing anything—especially origami—is to practice, practice, practice. Then, practice some more!

Now you're ready to learn and perfect one of the most beautiful and original art forms around. You'll learn basic folds and forms that are used throughout all 50 origami projects. Then you'll discover fun ways to show off your art as centerpieces, room decorations, and much more!

Getting Started with Origami

To some people this may look like nothing more than a stack of paper. To those who can perform the ancient oriental art of origami, this stack can be a barnyard full of animals, a fleet of boats sailing on a paper ocean, or even a spacecraft rocketing through a field of paper stars. No matter what you choose to make, origami is an adventure. Let's begin by looking at the basics.

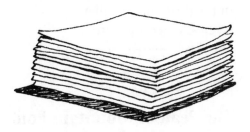

Basic Materials

A few of the designs in this section require the use of scissors, but generally the only material you will need is paper. Any thin, square paper will do, but special origami paper is available at art supply and specialty stores. It is colored on one side, white on the other, and precut into squares. Once the form is complete, you can sketch on details or use glitter, feathers, cotton wool, or other materials to make your creation unique. Let your imagination go!

Basic Folds

The figures in this section are accompanied by written instructions and diagrams to help you through each step. Simply follow the direction of the arrow when making your fold. There are two basic folds that you will need to know:

The Valley Fold

Fold the paper toward you.
In the diagrams, a valley fold
is represented by a line
like this: — — — — — — —

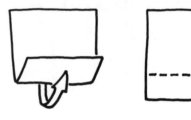

The Peak or Mountain Fold

Fold the paper away from you.
In the diagrams, a peak or mountain
fold is represented by a line
like this: —··—·—··—·—··—

IMPORTANT TIP!

When making your origami figures, remember that neatness counts! *Always* work on a smooth, hard surface and make each crease as even and crisp as possible. Sharp creases make the form easier to work with and they make your finished project look better. If you make a mistake, start over with a fresh piece of paper.

Basic Forms

The following forms are the basis for many different figures. They are listed here in order of difficulty, from beginner to advanced. Take some time to practice and get used to these forms. Some are more challenging than others, but once you master the basics, you will be ready to create the 50 nifty figures in this section or even design some of your own. The 50 nifty origami crafts begin on page 178. Happy folding!

Basic Form 1

1. Begin with a square piece of paper in a flat diamond shape. Note that in the diagram the corners are labeled A and B. Fold your paper in half as shown, bringing point A to meet point B. Make a sharp crease across the fold, then reopen it into a square.

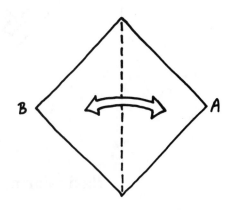

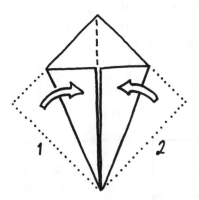

2. Now fold sides 1 and 2 to the center line. Your paper should look like a kite.

Basic Form 2

1. Begin with a square piece of paper in a flat diamond shape. Fold your paper in half as shown, bringing point A to meet point B, and make a sharp crease.

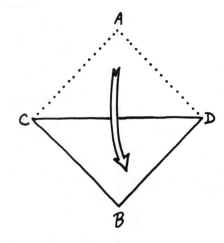

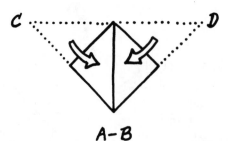

2. Now fold points C and D to meet points A-B and the form is complete.

Basic Form 3

1. Begin with a square piece of paper. Fold the paper in half from side to side, then top to bottom to form the creases shown. Then reopen it into a square.

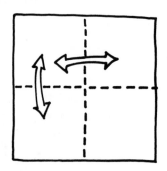

2. Next, fold points A and B to the center.

3. Finally, fold points C and D to the center.

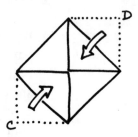

Basic Form 4

1. First, complete the instructions for Basic Form 1, then fold points C and D (at the wide end of the kite) to the center line and make two sharp creases. Now fold the form in half, bringing point E to meet point F.

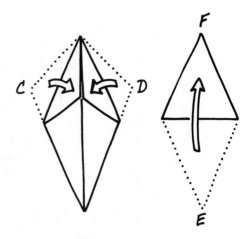

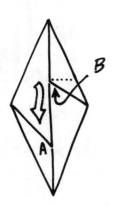 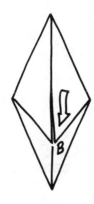

2. Carefully open the form back to a kite. Then, while holding down point B with your fingertip, lift point A up and fold it toward the center line. Repeat the same fold with point B.

Basic Form 5

1. Begin with a square piece of paper. Fold your paper in half from side to side. Next, open the paper to a square, then fold it from top to bottom. Reopen the paper and fold it diagonally both ways. Now when you reopen the paper to a square you should have the pattern of creases shown in the illustration.

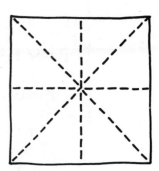

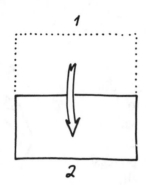

2. Fold down side 1 to meet side 2.

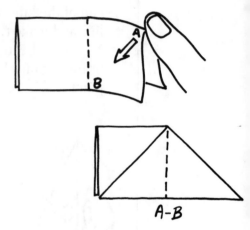

3. Hold the right side of the form open at point A, then push down on it to meet point B, making a flat triangle.

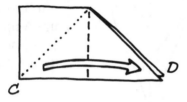

4. Fold point C to meet point D.

5. Repeat steps 3 and 4 with the left side and your form is ready.

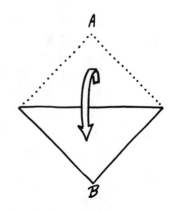

Basic Form 6

1. Begin with step 1 of Basic Form 5.

2. Turn the paper to form a diamond shape, then fold point A to meet point B.

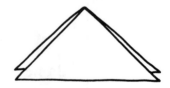

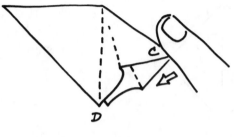

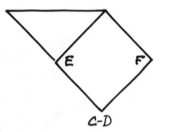

3. Carefully hold the right side of the form open at point C, then push down on it to meet point D, making a flat diamond shape.

4. Fold point E to meet point F.

5. Repeat steps 3 and 4 with the left side of the form.

Basic Form 7

1. To make this form you must first follow all of the steps in Basic Form 6.

2. Using only the top layer of paper, fold points A and B to the center line, then fold down point C. Remember to make those creases sharp and crisp!

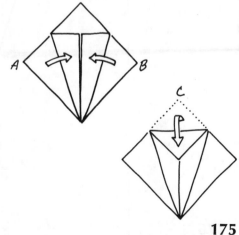

175

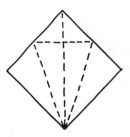

3. This part is easy. Just unfold the form back to a small diamond, as in step 1.

4. This part is a little tougher, but don't get discouraged. First, lift up point D (top layer only), fold it back, then flatten it into a long diamond shape.

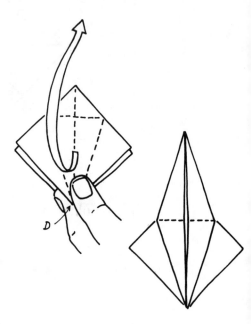

5. Turn the form over and repeat steps 2 through 4.

Basic Form 8

1. Begin this form with step 1 of Basic Form 5, then fold sides 1 and 2 toward the center line.

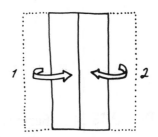

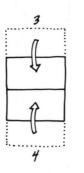 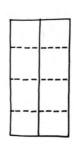

2. Now fold sides 3 and 4 up to the center line. Make a nice, sharp crease, then unfold it.

3. Next, you must make two diagonal creases across the center. Do this by first folding point A to meet point B. Crease the paper sharply, then unfold it. Now repeat this step on the opposite side, bringing point C to meet point D.

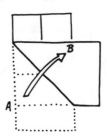 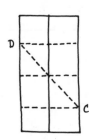

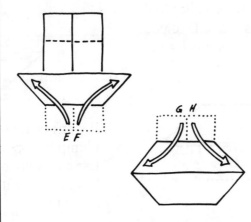

4. This step might take some practice. Lift points E and F up and out, then flatten the form. Repeat this step with points G and H and this tricky form is finished.

This Little Piggy

Here's a fine, plump pig to begin a barnyard scene. It's complete with a flat pig snout. Going one step further will give your pig a curly tail to wiggle, too.

Directions

1. Begin with a square and fold sides 1 and 2 to the center, then turn the form over and fold sides 3 and 4 to the center.

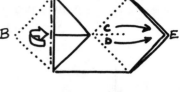

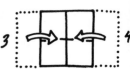

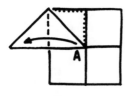

2. Next, pull out point A on the upper left square as shown, and flatten it into a triangle. Now repeat this step with each of the squares.

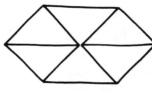

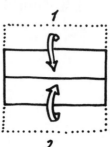

3. Using a mountain fold, turn back point B. Use a valley fold to bring points C and D to point E, then fold back points F and G.

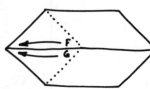

4. It won't be long now before your plump little porker takes shape. Use a mountain fold to fold the form in half with the opening at the top.

5. With the longer side of the form facing down, you're ready to make the legs by folding point H (front flap only) forward and point I (front flap only) back as shown.

6. Now fold point I down, then repeat steps 5 and 6 on the back of the form.

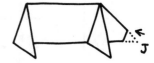

7. There's only one more thing to do: Tuck in point J to make the pig's flat snout.

One Step Further

What You'll Need:
glue • marking pen • curling ribbon

Draw eyes and a mouth on your pig. Make its curly tail by gluing on about an inch of curling ribbon.

Down on the Farm

With its peaked roof and wide door, this barn sets the scene for all of the origami chickens and pigs you'll create.

Directions

1. Begin with Basic Form 5, then fold point A and point C up to meet point B. Turn the form over and repeat this step with the remaining layer.

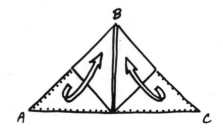

2. You now have a diamond shape. Fold this in half to make a crease and unfold, then lift up the triangle on the right side and push on point A to form a square.

 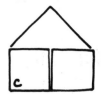

3. Lift up the triangle on the left side and push on point C to form a square. Then turn the form over and repeat steps 3 and 4 on the other side.

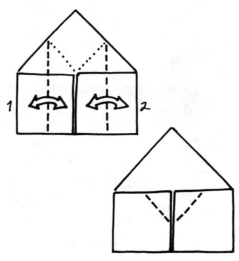

4. Fold outside edges 1 and 2 to the center to make a crease, then unfold them again. Follow this by folding and unfolding triangle shapes on each "door" to make creases as shown.

5. To create the large front door, fold point A to meet point D, and point C to meet point E.

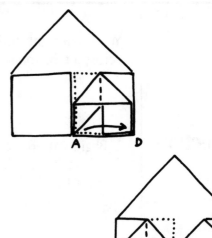

6. To finish, fold up the center triangle.

One Step Further

What You'll Need:
shoebox lid ● sand ● Popsicle® sticks ● mirror

To create a mini-barnyard, stand your barn in the center of a shoebox lid. Popsicle sticks glued to the inside edge of the lid make a perfect fence. Fill the lid with sand for your paper pigs to root in. You can even lay a small mirror in the box to serve as a tiny pond for birds to bathe in!

Super Simple Sailboat

You'll sail right through folding this little boat and in no time launch it across a tabletop sea.

Directions

1. Begin with Basic Form 1 and fold points A and B back to meet sides 1 and 2.

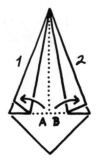

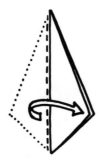

2. Use a valley fold to fold the form in half and create your sail.

3. To make the base of the boat, fold up point C in a valley fold, crease, and unfold. Then turn up point C to form a "pocket" around point D.

4. To make your boat "seaworthy," fold back point E as shown and set your sails!

Hatful of Fun

By using paper of different sizes, you can make a hat to fit anyone. Use gift-wrapping paper to make a hat for any occasion!

Directions

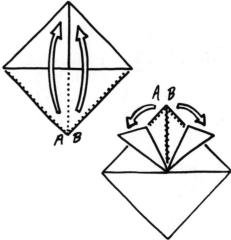

1. Begin with Basic Form 2 and fold up the front flaps only of points A and B, then fold points A and B back as shown.

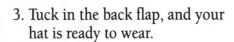

2. Now fold the front flap only of point C in the direction of the arrow, then fold up side 1.

3. Tuck in the back flap, and your hat is ready to wear.

One Step Further

What You'll Need:
glue • glitter • confetti

Make a fashion statement! Decorate the finished hat by gluing on glitter or confetti.

Toadless Toadstool

Whether you call it a toadstool or a mushroom, if you use your imagination you can picture a tiny elf perched under this origami creation.

Directions

1. Begin with Basic Form 3 and unfold the bottom triangle. Use a valley fold to fold down side 1, then turn the form over.

2. The cap of your toadstool is easy to make. Simply fold points A and B in valley folds to the center line.

3. Now reach inside the triangle on the upper right and fold the inside flap only to the center line. Repeat this step with the triangle on the upper left side of the form.

4. Here's the last step. Make small valley folds at the top and bottom of the form and turn it over to see the finished toadstool. Add different-sized dots to your toadstool for a spotty look!

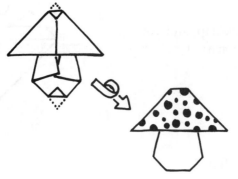

Angelic Origami

How can paper be angelic? You'll see when you fold this lovely origami angel, which can stand in a window or on a mantel as a perfect holiday decoration.

Directions

1. Begin with Basic Form 2, with the opening in the back. Then fold points A and B to the center line.

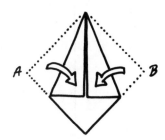

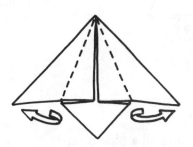

2. Next, unfold the back flaps. These will soon be the angel's wings.

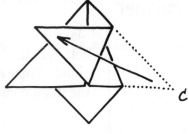

3. Now fold point C over to the left and crease it well, then fold it back to the right as shown.

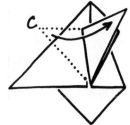

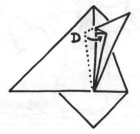

4. You now have a little flap across the center line. This is point D. Use a valley fold to fold it in the same direction as point C.

5. Repeat steps 3 and 4 on the left side of the form, then turn the form over.

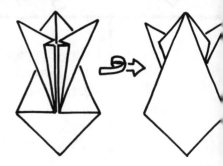

6. To give your angel heavenly detail, fold in points E and F as shown. Use a mountain fold to turn back point G. This flap wi allow your angel to stand.

One Step Further

What You'll Need:
glue • glitter • cotton ball • pipe cleaner

Make your angel sparkle by gluing glitter to the wings. Then spread cotton at the base so that your angel appears to be standing on a fluffy cloud. Finally, bend a pipe cleaner into a small circle at one end. Glue the straight end to the back of your angel and presto, she's got a halo!

A Tisket, a Tasket

Your friends will love this special bird basket!

Directions

1. Begin with Basic Form 1 and fold points A and B to the center.

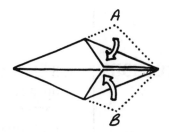

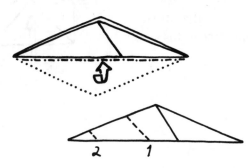

2. Now use a mountain fold to fold the form in half with the opening at the top, then fold and unfold the paper to make two creases as shown.

3. Tuck in fold 1 to create the bird's long neck.

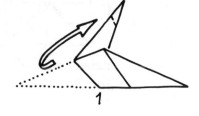

4. Finally, tuck in fold 2 to form its slender beak.

One Step Further

What You'll Need:
marking pen • name tags • party candy

During a party, this lovely bird basket can be perched at each guest's place setting. Tuck a name tag into the fold at the bird's back or, for a special treat, fill the basket with candy.

The Great Frame Fold-Up!

Here's the perfect way to show off your favorite photos.

Directions

1. Begin with Basic Form 3 with the open side down. Fold all four corners to the center, then turn the form over and repeat this step.

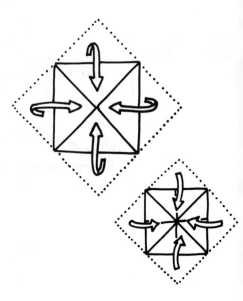

2. Now turn the form over again and lift point A up and out to form a square, as shown in the illustration. Repeat this step at each corner, then turn the form over once again.

3. Unfold point B (top flap only) from the center as shown, then repeat this step at each corner, then . . . you guessed it! Turn the form over.

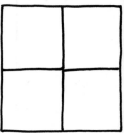

4. The final step is to slip your snapshot into the square at the center of your new paper frame!

One Step Further

What You'll Need:
cardboard • scissors • glue

Make your creation stand by cutting a piece of cardboard the same size as your frame. Cut a two-inch-wide strip of cardboard that is half that length. Finally, glue the strip to the center of the cardboard square for support and glue your frame to the front of the square.

Cozy Cottage

There's no place like home, and no easier way to build your cozy cottage than with these few steps.

1. Begin with a square and fold sides 1 and 2 to the center.

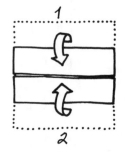

2. Next, turn the form over and fold sides 3 and 4 to the center.

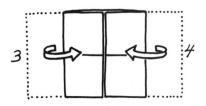

3. To build the roof, pull out point A on the upper left square as shown in the illustration, then flatten it into a triangle.

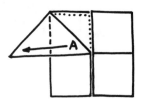

4. Repeat step 3 with the upper right square, turn the form over, and you're almost ready to move in!

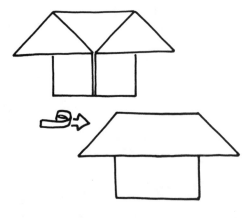

One Step Further

What You'll Need:
marking pen • cotton ball • green food coloring • glue

Complete your home by drawing a door and windows. You can do a little landscaping, too. Start by adding one or two drops of green food coloring to a cup of water. Lightly dip a small cotton ball into the water, allow the ball to dry, then glue it near the door of your house to create a tiny green bush!

Perfect Pinwheel

This pinwheel can be lots of fun on a windy day.

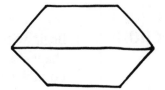

1. Begin with Basic Form 8.

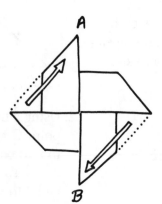

2. Fold point A up and B down as shown and you have a pinwheel. Wasn't that easy?

One Step Further

What You'll Need:
tack ● two Popsicle® sticks ● glue

To make your pinwheel work, glue the two Popsicle sticks together to serve as a handle. Now stick a small tack through the center of the pinwheel and secure it lightly to the handle. Use a double pinwheel to dress up the design. Now wait for the wind or just blow, blow, blow!

A "Neat" Neat Coaster

Have you ever picked up a glass to find that it has left behind a wet ring on your table? Since neatness counts, follow these simple directions and turn two small squares of paper into a really neat coaster.

Directions

1. Begin with paper in a diamond shape, fold it in half, then fold point A (front flap only) to meet point B. Complete this step by turning the form over and repeating the fold on the other side.

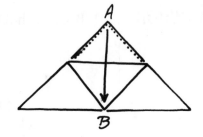

2. Using a mountain fold, fold back point C, while using a valley fold to fold point D forward. You now have form 1. Repeat steps 1 and 2 to make form 2.

3. Follow the illustration and slip the tip of form 1 into the pocket of form 2 and the tip of form 2 into the pocket of form 1 . . . and there you are!

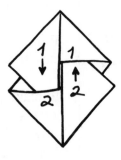

One Step Further

What You'll Need:
gift-wrapping paper • scissors

You can decorate a party table with these coasters. Make place mats by using large sheets cut from wrapping paper.

Creative Candle Cradle

Can a piece of paper be strong enough to support a candle? It can if you fold it the origami way. For a festive candleholder, make this form with foil-backed origami paper from the art- or craft-supply store. On page 195, you'll find directions for folding an origami candle to complete the mood.

Directions

1. Begin with Basic Form 3 with the open side down, and fold points A, B, C, and D to the center.

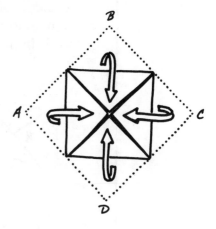

2. Carefully fold points A, B, C, and D back to meet the outside edges of the form.

3. So far so good? Then on to the next step. Using a mountain fold, fold the form in half, then push points A and C toward the center and tuck them in as shown.

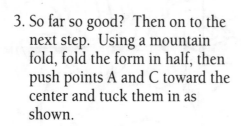

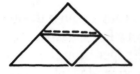

4. Be sure your form is nice and flat, then fold and unfold the top to make a sharp crease.

5. Open the form loosely and push the middle of the "star" down and in to form a four-pointed "bowl" in the center.

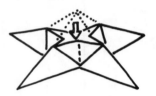

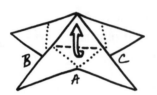

6. Finally, unfold points A, B, C, and D.

A Clever Candle

Here's a candle that is always lit but never melts. It is the perfect match for the origami candle holder on page 193.

Directions

1. Begin with paper in a square. First, fold points A and B to the center line, then use mountain folds to fold back sides 1 and 2 to the center line.

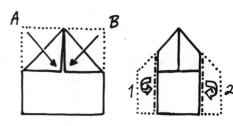

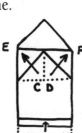

2. Fold points C and D to meet E and F, then use a valley fold to fold up side 3 about one quarter of an inch.

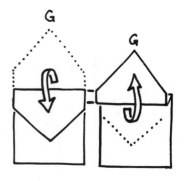

3. Turn the form over and fold point G down, then fold point G up again part way as shown in the illustration.

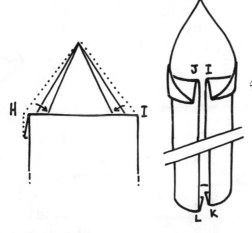

4. Turn the form over once more. Fold down points H and I, then "round out" your candle by bringing the sides together and inserting point I into point J, and K into L.

5. You won't need a match to light this candle. Just twist the pointed tip of the paper to form the flame.

Wrap It Up

Here's a way to make a small gift even more special—present it in a box that you created yourself.

Directions

1. Begin with your paper in a square. Fold the top and bottom of the paper to the center, then fold all four corners in as shown.

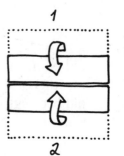

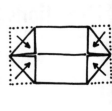

2. Find points A and B. Fold them both toward the center, make a nice sharp crease, and unfold them again.

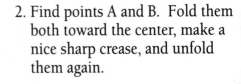

3. Ready for the next step? Open the upper left corner to form a square, then pull point C up and across as shown. Repeat this step with the other three corners. Finally, use mountain folds to fold back sides 1 and 2, crease, then unfold.

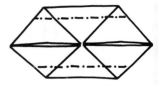

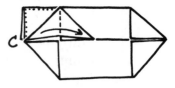

4. Here's where you have to pay close attention! Put your index fingers above the crease (heavy line) on side 1 and your thumbs below the crease. Use the illustration as a guide. Firmly pinch the paper together. This will form one side of your box.

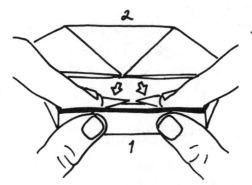

5. By repeating step 4 on side 2, sides 3 and 4 will naturally be drawn up. Simply tuck them into place and your box is almost ready.

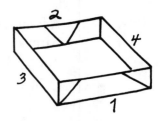

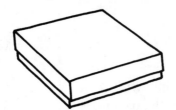

6. Make a top for your box by using a slightly larger piece of paper and following steps 1 through 5.

A Real Clucker

A farm scene would not be complete without a chubby hen in the barnyard. If you use one large piece of origami paper and several smaller ones, you can create a whole family of chickens!

Directions

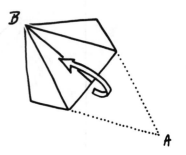

1. Begin the mother hen with Basic Form 1, then turn the paper over and fold point A to meet point B.

2. Now fold point A back again. About half of the triangle should overlap past the edge of the paper.

3. Next, turn the form over and fold point B to meet point C. Once that step is complete, fold point A toward point C (it will not quite reach point C).

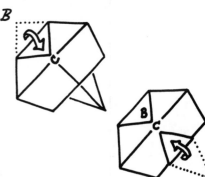

4. To make the hen's sharp beak, fold point A back again about two-thirds of the way, so the points overlap the edge.

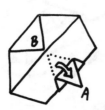

5. The body will begin to take shape when you use a valley fold to bring point D to meet point E.

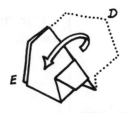

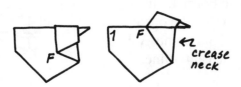

6. Pull up on the hen's head until point F is even with line 1, then crease the neck as shown in the illustration.

7. Finally pull the beak down into position. Repeat the above steps using smaller pieces of paper to create the mother hen's baby chicks.

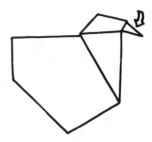

One Step Further

What You'll Need:
glue • feathers • pencil

With a little imagination, you can really bring your chicken family to life. Glue feathers on the tails, wings, and wherever else you want. Draw eyes on each little critter.

A Whale of an Idea

By using a large square of gift-wrapping paper, you can make a really big whale. Then go one step further so you can yell, "Thar she blows!"

Directions

1. Begin with Basic Form 4. Turn the form over so that the opening is on the back. Fold points A, B, and C toward the center line.

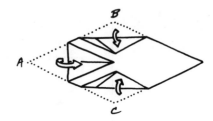

2. Fold the paper down so that lines 1 and 2 meet, then fold back the whale's fins.

3. Now make the creases as shown near point D. While holding the tail just below the first crease, spread the tip open and up.

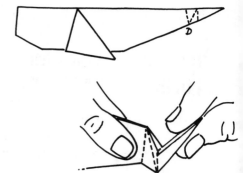

One Step Further

What You'll Need:
cotton ball • paper clip

You can make your whale appear to be spouting. Tear a small amount of material from the cotton ball and spread it out. Twist the bottom half to form a stem. Paper-clip the stem into the opening in the paper above the whale's head.

Chattering Bird

With your help, this bird will flap its wings and open and close its beak. You can almost hear it chattering.

Directions

1. Begin with Basic Form 4 and fold point A to meet point B. This will make a triangle with two smaller triangles inside.

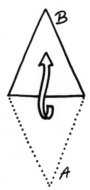

2. Gently grasp the tips of each of the smaller triangles and pull them out to the sides. Once you have a shape that looks something like a crown, fold and unfold the form, creasing it as shown.

3. To give the bird a beak, simply fold point A toward you and point B away from you. Crease the paper sharply, then unfold point B.

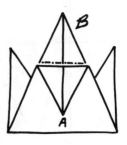

4. Fold and unfold both halves of the beak to make the creases shown in the illustration.

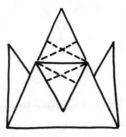

5. Finally, fold the wings away from you until they meet. As you do this the beak will start to close. Pull carefully on the ends of the beak until the form is flat.

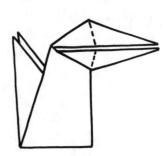

Precious Pup/Cuddly Kitty

This form is actually two-faced! Fold your paper into a floppy-eared puppy, or turn it over, make a few different folds, and presto—you've created a cat! You'll need a pen to draw in your new pets' faces.

Directions

1. First, form a triangle with the fold at the top by folding the paper in half and bringing point A to meet point B.

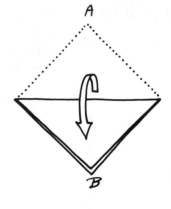

2. To form the puppy's floppy ears, fold points C and D down, then fold points A-B and point E back and the pup's head will take shape. Finish your puppy by drawing eyes, a nose, and a little mouth.

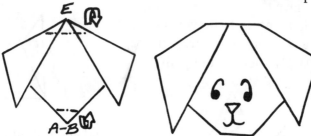

One Step Further

You can use this design to make a cuddly kitty by following steps 1 and 2. Then turn the form over and around so that the ears point up. Now fold back points A-B and your kitty is ready for eyes, nose, and a mouth—and don't forget the whiskers.

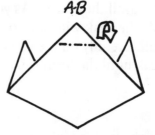

Paper Pest

This little fly won't bother anyone—it doesn't buzz around, and it will never land where it isn't invited.

Directions

1. Begin with Basic Form 2 (with the open points at the top). Fold points A and B about halfway down to make the fly's wings.

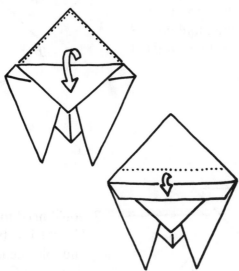

2. Now there are two triangular flaps pointing up. Fold only the front flap down not quite halfway to form a triangle, then fold the base of this triangle down, even with the wings.

3. Is your fly starting to bug you yet? Give it shape by using mountain folds to turn the sides under.

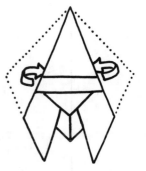

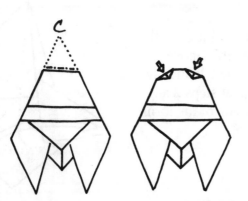

4. To complete the paper pest, form the head by folding point C under, then fold both corners back to give your fly real bug eyes.

203

Flashy Fighter Jet

You won't need a model airplane kit to turn an ordinary piece of paper into "fly" paper.

Directions

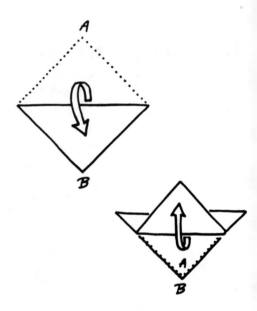

1. To prepare for take-off, form a triangle by folding point A to meet point B, then fold point A back again about two-thirds of the way up.

2. You'll need to concentrate here. Use the illustration as a guide and fold the left corner over so that point C touches line 2, then fold the left side over to meet the midline crease.

3. Are you ready to manufacture the wings? Lift point C on the left side of the form, move it gently back to the left and lay it flat, then repeat steps 2 and 3 on the right side of the form.

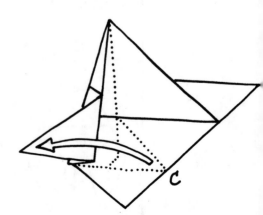

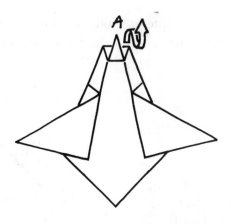

4. To make the needle nose of the plane, fold point A down in a valley fold, then back in a mountain fold as shown.

5. You're almost ready to start your engines! Using a valley fold, fold the model in half.

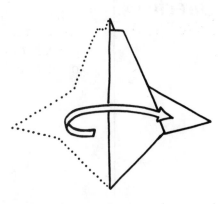

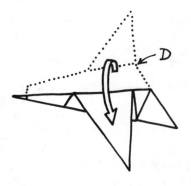

6. Fold down one wing so that point D meets the bottom fold.

7. Turn the form over and repeat step 6. Now spread out the wings and you're ready to soar!

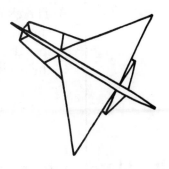

Cute Cup

This paper cup is very simple to make, but it can come in handy to hold candy, pebbles, paper clips, and maybe even a few sips of water. But drink fast!

Directions

1. Begin the form with a triangle (fold at the bottom) by folding the paper in half and bringing point A to meet point B.

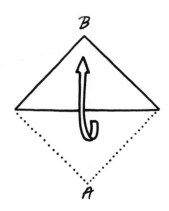

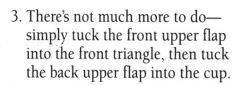

2. Fold point C to meet point D, and point E to meet point F.

3. There's not much more to do—simply tuck the front upper flap into the front triangle, then tuck the back upper flap into the cup.

One Step Further

What You'll Need:
string • sharp pencil or scissors

Turn your cup into a tiny purse or baby bucket! Just poke a hole in both sides of the cup with a sharp pencil or the tip of your scissors. Now pull string through each hole and make a knot on each end, and you'll have a handle to carry your load!

Handy Holder

Things are easier to find if you have a special place to put them. Here is a design for a handy holder that will keep all of your pencils, marbles, or precious keepsakes within easy reach.

Directions

1. Begin with Basic Form 5, open end up, then fold over point A (front flap only).

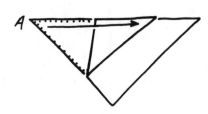

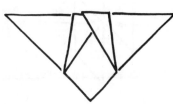

2. Now fold point A back and tuck the tip inside the top of the form. Repeat steps 1 and 2 with the left side of the form, then turn the form over and repeat steps 1 and 2 with both sides.

3. Here's the final step. Fold point B up and back to make a sharp crease. Gently slip your finger inside and open the holder while flattening the base at point B.

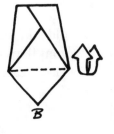

One Step Further

What You'll Need:
scissors • cardboard

To make your handy holder strong, cut a square of cardboard that is slightly smaller than the base. Slip the square inside and to the bottom of the form to act as a support. Now put your treasures inside!

Hot-Air Balloon

You won't need a string to keep your paper balloon in place, but you will have to blow it up.

Directions

1. Begin with Basic Form 5 and fold points A and B (front flaps only) to the center, then turn the form over and repeat step 1.

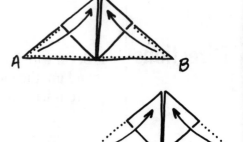

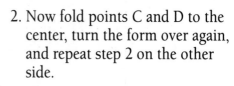

2. Now fold points C and D to the center, turn the form over again, and repeat step 2 on the other side.

3. Fold and unfold points E and F (front flaps only) to make a sharp crease.

4. Next, tuck points E and F into the center triangles as shown, then turn your form over and repeat step 3 on the other side.

5. Finally, blow into the hole at the bottom of the form and your balloon will inflate before your eyes.

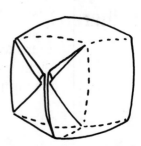

The Flying Crane

A traditional origami form, the flying crane is challenging to fold, but it's worth the effort.

Directions

1. Begin with Basic Form 7, with the two open points facing down.

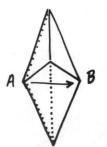 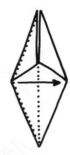

2. Fold point A (front flap only) to meet point B. Turn the form over and repeat this step.

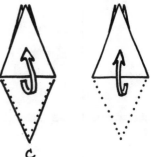

3. Now fold up point C (front flap only), then turn the form over and repeat this step.

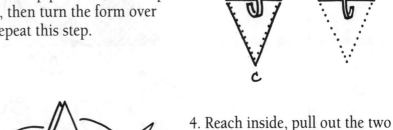

4. Reach inside, pull out the two inner points, flatten the form, and it will look like a three-pointed crown.

5. You're getting close. Make a crease in point 1, then tuck in the paper to form the crane's head.

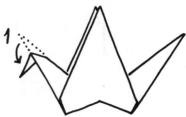

6. The last step is to make the wings curve slightly. Roll each wing around a pencil, then unroll them, and your crane is ready for flight.

One Step Further

In one hand, hold your crane at its base. With your other hand, move the tail toward the head, then back again. The crane will flap its wide wings.

The Star Attraction

You'll shine when you show your friends this four-pointed star. It's fun to make and is a perfect decoration for holiday packages.

Directions

1. Begin with Basic Form 7 with the two open points up. Fold point A (front flap only) up to meet points B and C.

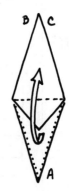

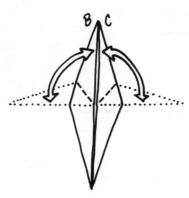

2. Then turn the form over and fold and unfold points B and C to make creases as shown.

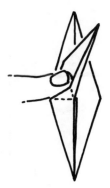

3. Now lift the left triangle until it is at a right angle to the form. Slip your finger into the opening on the side of the raised triangle. Open it slightly.

4. On the center of the star, push down and out to flatten the left triangle. Repeat this step on the right side of the form and your heavenly star is finished.

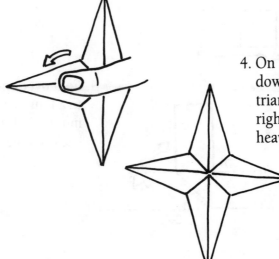

211

26

Friendship Ring

With one piece of paper you can make a matching pair of rings—one for you and one for a friend.

Directions

1. Begin by sharply creasing your paper in the center and tearing it into two equal pieces. You will be using one half-sheet for each ring you make.

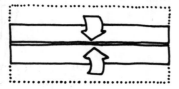

2. Now hold one of the halves of paper lengthwise, fold the outer edges into the center, then fold the paper once more to make a long, thin strip.

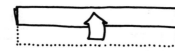

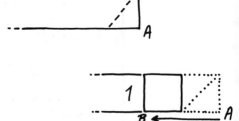

3. At one end of the strip, fold and unfold point A, then fold down side 1 to form a square so that point A meets point B.

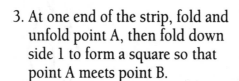

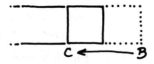

4. Fold over one more time, unfold to a long strip again, then use a mountain fold to turn point C back to meet point D as shown.

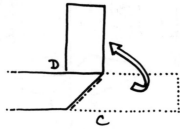

5. Use a mountain fold again to fold point E back to meet point F. You will find that you have formed a thick triangle at the back of your ring and your paper should look like an L on its side.

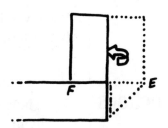

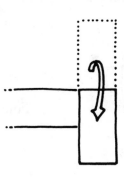

6. Now use a valley fold to fold the upper leg of the L down.

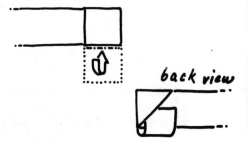

back view

7. Tuck the lower square behind the form and into the triangle at the back of the ring.

8. Finally, fold back the corners at the long end of the strip, curl it around, and tuck it into the open end of the square. If your ring is too large, cut some length off of the long end of the strip before you tuck it in. Now use the other half of your paper to make a matching ring for your special friend.

Fluttering Butterfly

Use several sheets of paper of different colors to make a bevy of beautiful butterflies.

Directions

1. Begin with Basic Form 8 and use a mountain fold to fold the form in half, open side up.

2. Fold points A and B down as shown.

3. Finally, turn the form over, then fold it in half and unfold it to make a sharp crease between the butterfly's wings. Turn out points C and D to give the back of each wing more shape.

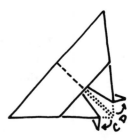

One Step Further

What You'll Need:
pipe cleaners • glue

Glue pipe cleaners to your butterfly to serve as its body and antennae.

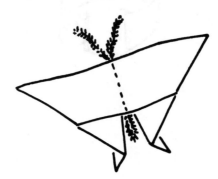

A Real Turtleneck

It may not cross the finish line in any races, but this turtle will still be a winner with one sheet of paper, a pair of scissors, and your creativity.

Directions

1. Begin with Basic Form 2 and fold points A and B (front flaps only) up to meet point C.

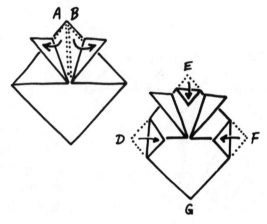

2. Fold A and B down as shown, then fold down points D, E, and F.

3. Are your scissors on hand? Fold point E up again about halfway. Next, make a small cut in the center (front flap only) above point G.

 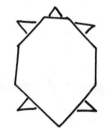

4. Finally, fold out the two flaps made by cutting the paper. Turn the form over and your turtle is complete.

One Step Further

What You'll Need:
glitter • sequins • glue • safety pin

Decorate your turtle's shell with glitter or sequins. You can wear your creation as a pin by gluing a safety pin to the back side!

A Terrific Teddy

Once you've followed these few simple steps, you'll have a little critter cute enough to give a big bear hug, especially if you glue on tiny button eyes!

Directions

1. Begin with Basic Form 2 and fold up points A and B (front flaps only) to meet point C.

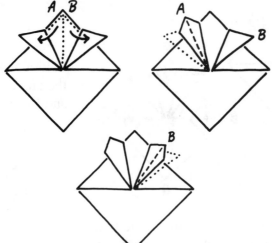

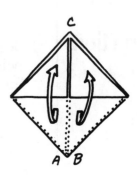

2. Now fold A and B down as shown, then lift point A up at a right angle to the form and press down to flatten it. Repeat this step with point B.

3. Fold down points D, E, and F, then turn the form over.

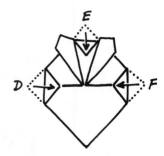

4. To make your bear's nose, fold point G (front flap only) up, then back a little.

5. The last step is to tuck the back flap of point G inside the form, and your bear is done.

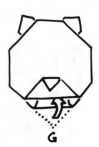

A Super Seal

Create a seashore scene with this super seal at center stage.

Directions

1. Begin with Basic Form 4, with the open-ended flaps pointing to the left. Then use a mountain fold to fold the form in half, bringing point B to meet point A.

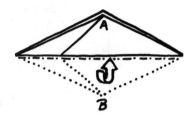

2. Fold point C back and down as shown in the illustration on both the front and back sides of the form, but don't turn the form over.

3. Next, fold and unfold both ends of the form to make the creases for the neck and tail.

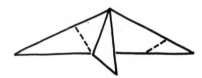

4. Take a moment to study the illustration. Now place your finger in the opening at the top of the form, then tuck the paper in at both folds to create the neck and the tail.

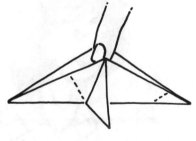

5. Making the head and snout is similar to step 4. This time fold and unfold the paper to make the creases as shown on the seal's neck.

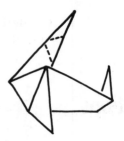

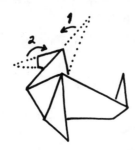

6. Tuck the paper in at crease 1 to make the head. Make the flattened snout by tucking in crease 2.

One Step Further

What You'll Need:
shoebox lid • sand • pebbles • small rocks

To display your seal, fill a shoebox lid with sand and small pebbles. Give the seal a place to rest by adding a small, flat rock to your seashore scene.

⟨31⟩ Paper Pocket

If you use a large piece of paper, you can make an innovative envelope to hold all of those special deliveries your mail carrier brings.

Directions

1. Begin by using a valley fold to make a crease in the center of a square of paper. Next, fold sides 1 and 2 to meet at the crease.

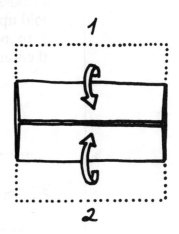

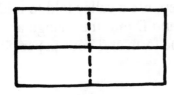

2. Using the valley fold again, fold and unfold to make a crease in the center. Then fold sides 3 and 4 to meet at the center line. Unfold your form again and you will have three sharp creases.

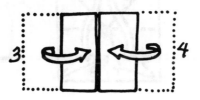

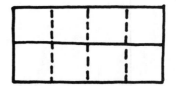

3. Now, fold down points A and B, fold in sides 3 and 4, then fold up points C and D to make a crease, then unfold them.

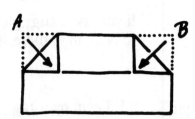

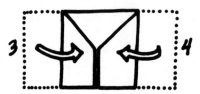 

4. For the final step, use a valley fold to fold the form in half. Tuck points C and D into the triangular pockets in the upper half of the form and your paper pocket is complete.

Star Quality

You'll twinkle with delight when you've completed this nifty star box for storing your favorite treasures.

Directions

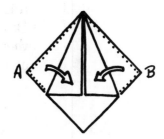

1. Begin your star box with Basic Form 6. Be sure the open end is up, then fold points A and B (front flaps only) to the center.

2. Firmly fold and unfold points C and D to make the creases as shown. Now lift the left "wing" of the triangle, open it slightly, and press down on point C to flatten it, then repeat this step with point D, turn the form over, and repeat this step on the other side.

3. Now you are ready to grasp point E (front flap only) and use a mountain fold to fold it back into the center. Repeat this step with point F, then turn the form over and repeat this step on the opposite side.

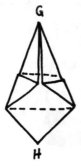

4. Using valley folds, fold and unfold points G and H to make sharp creases.

5. At the top of the form are four open points. To make the star box, take the shape, grasp the two outer points, and pull outward.

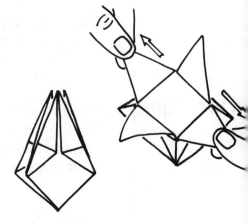

6. Flatten the base and your star box is complete.

One Step Further

This little box is an excellent way to present holiday candies. For a special New Year's treat, fill it with glitter or confetti to throw when the clock strikes midnight.

Sly Fox

You'll look pretty sly when you show your friends how your pointy-eared fox appears to bark!

Directions

1. Begin by folding a square of paper in half as shown.

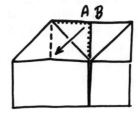

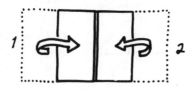

2. Next, fold sides 1 and 2 to the center line, then fold down points A and B.

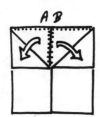

3. Now lift point A open. Push down to flatten it, then repeat this step with point B.

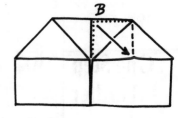

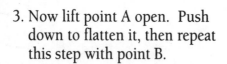

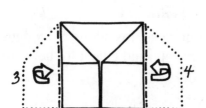

4. Use mountain folds to turn back sides 3 and 4.

5. Fold up point C (front flap only), then turn the form over and repeat this step on the opposite side.

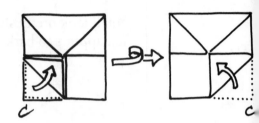

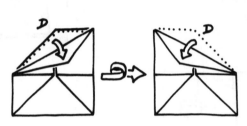

6. Although it may not look like a fox yet, your form is almost ready. Fold up point D (front flap only), then turn the form over and repeat this step on the other side.

7. Now slip your fingertips into the opening and pull the sides outward. Your fox will appear when you tuck in and close its mouth.

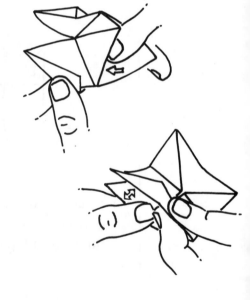

One Step Further

What You'll Need:
scissors • glue • red felt

How about giving your clever fox a long red tongue? Cut a small piece of felt into the proper shape and glue it to the bottom of the animal's open mouth.

Paper Pine Tree

You won't need water or soil to grow this paper pine tree, just your own nimble fingers. Why not fold a few and create a fabulous forest! You might pick a special one to write a holiday greeting on. Slip it in a paper pocket from page 219 and give it to a friend!

Directions

1. Begin each tree with Basic Form 4, then fold point A up as shown.

2. Now fold point A down again but not quite all the way.

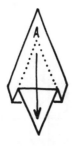

3. One more time! Fold point A up about halfway and your first tree is complete. What could be easier?!

 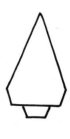

Under the Big Top!

Use colorful paper to make this cheerful circus tent. A large square of gift-wrapping paper with stripes is perfect!

Directions

1. Begin with your paper in a square. Fold sides 1 and 2 about half an inch in from the outside. If you're using a larger-than-average piece of paper, fold the sides in even more. Then use a valley fold to fold the form in half, bringing side 3 to meet side 4.

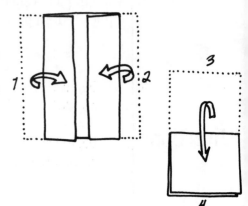

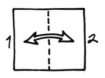

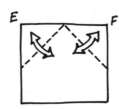

2. Now fold the form in half once more, this time bringing side 1 to meet side 2. Then unfold your form to make the crease as shown. You will need to make two more creases by folding and unfolding points E and F. If you make the creases sharp enough, the next step will be simple.

3. First, open the right side slightly. Then push down on point F and tuck the fold inside. Repeat this step with point E and your tent is ready to raise!

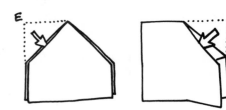

One Step Further

What You'll Need:
sawdust • shoebox lid • toothpicks • colored paper • scissors • glue

Set the background for the "Greatest Show on Earth" by filling a shoebox lid with sawdust. Then cut tiny flags from colored paper and glue them to toothpicks. Use the flags to decorate your circus tent.

Let's Make Music!

Here's a stand-up piano that will fit inside a notebook!

Directions

1. Begin with a square of paper and fold it in half from top to bottom, then fold the form in half once again, this time from side to side. Make a sharp crease, and unfold it.

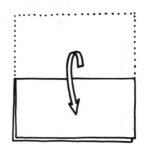

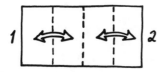

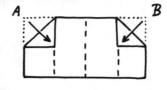

2. Carefully bring sides 1 and 2 into the center line. Make crisp, sharp creases and unfold them. Next, use the outer creases as a guide to fold points A and B down as shown.

3. This next step can be challenging, but work slowly and you will get it. Lift the right side up at a right angle to the form and push down on point B to flatten it. Repeat this step with point A on the left side of the form.

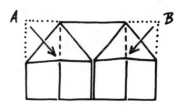

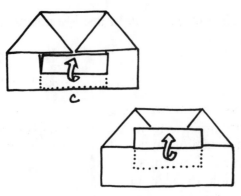

4. You are now ready to make the keyboard! Fold point C up so that it is level with the base of the triangles, then fold the same section of paper up one more time

5. Now bring the sides in and the keyboard down and your stand-up piano is ready to play!

One Step Further

What You'll Need:
fine-tipped marking pen • ruler

Add the finishing touch to your piano by neatly drawing in the keys. Make sure to use a ruler to make each line as straight as possible.

Peter Paper Cottontail

You will need a pair of scissors to make this bouncing bunny's long ears spring to life.

Directions

1. Begin with Basic Form 1 and fold point A toward point B, then back again about halfway.

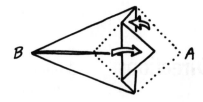

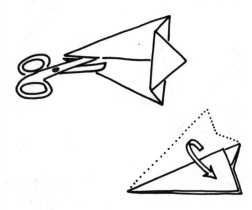

2. Do you have your scissors ready? Carefully make a cut like the one in the illustration. The length of the cut will be about one-third the size of your form, which you will then fold in half with a valley fold.

3. All that's left to do is to make the bunny's ears, and that's easily done by folding point B (front flap only) straight up. That's the first ear, and the second is made by doing the same thing to the back flap using a mountain fold.

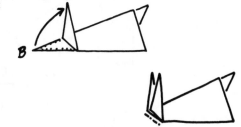

One Step Further

What You'll Need:
glue • cotton ball

Giving your bunny a fluffy tail is as easy as one, two, three. One—put a spot of glue on the rabbit's tail end. Two—form a cottontail to fit your bunny. Three—glue it in place to make a cottontail that really deserves its name!

The Crowning Touch

It doesn't take long to make this royal headgear fit for a king or queen!

Directions

1. Begin with Basic Form 2 and fold points A and B up.

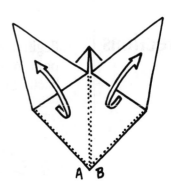

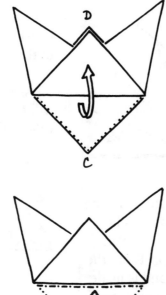

2. Now fold point C (front flap only) up to meet point D using a valley fold. Then use a mountain fold to fold the back flap at point C behind the form. Your crown is ready to wear!

One Step Further

What You'll Need:
glue • glitter • sequins

To make your coronation truly grand, decorate your crown with sequin gems and golden flecks of glitter. If you use a large piece of paper, you can perch your creation on your own head!

Beautiful Bird

This bird isn't very difficult to fold, but you will need scissors to make its lovely tail.

Directions

1. Begin with a square of paper and fold points A and B to the center, then use a valley fold to fold the form in half, bringing side 1 to meet side 2.

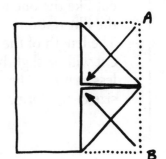

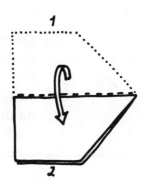

2. Next, make a sharp crease at point C, then tuck this point in to form the bird's head.

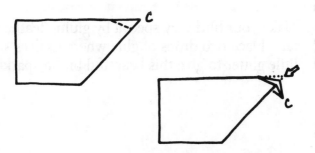

3. It's time to use your scissors. Carefully make a cut like the one in the illustration. The length of the cut will be slightly less that half the size of the form.

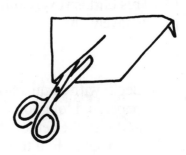

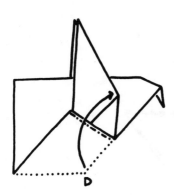

4. Once your cut is finished, use a valley fold to fold point D (front flap only) straight up. Do the same with the back flap, using a mountain fold, and your bird is ready for flight.

One Step Further

What You'll Need:

glue • feathers • scissors • glitter

Make your bird very special by gluing feathers to its wings and flowing tail. Place two drops of glue where its eyes should be and sprinkle on a little glitter to give this beautiful bird a sparkling gaze.

Rock-a-Bye Baby

This little baby comes wrapped in its own blanket.

Directions

1. Begin with Basic Form 1 and use a mountain fold to fold back point A.

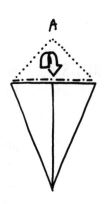

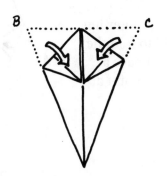

2. Next, fold points B and C to the center and turn your form over.

3. This part is a little tricky, so go slowly. Lift the upper square, reach inside, and fold points E and F to the center.

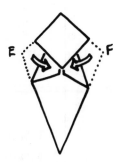

4. To complete your baby, fold back points G, H, and I, and get ready to sing a lullaby!

One Step Further

What You'll Need:
fine-tipped marker • yarn • ribbon

First, draw a face on your baby, then give it a few curls of yarn hair. If it is a little girl you may want to add a ribbon.

Here Comes Santa Claus!

It only takes a few simple folds to make this jolly fellow!

Directions

1. Start with Basic Form 1. Be sure the open side is down and toward the back. Carefully fold points A and B to the center line and use a valley fold to fold the form in half. You will have a triangle with the open point at the top.

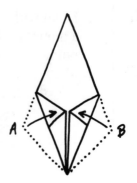

2. Fold the flaps at point C down so that the points just touch side 1.

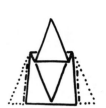

3. You're almost finished. Make Santa's pointed hat by lifting point C (this time the front flap only) and folding it back—but not quite all the way. Fold back both sides using mountain folds and Santa will appear.

One Step Further

What You'll Need:
cotton ball ● glue ● fine-tipped marker

Draw in Santa's face and glue on a cotton wool beard. You might want to add a little cotton trim around his hat and a pom-pom at the very top. Ho ho ho!

Sitting Pretty Puppy

This is a two-part form. To make this pleasant puppy you will need to add the form for Precious Pup on page 202. When it is complete, this puppy will always sit when it's told.

Directions

1. Make your puppy's body by folding a square of paper in half to form a triangle.

2. To make its wagging tail, fold back point A as shown in the illustration.

3. Now slip Precious Pup's head onto its body. Wasn't that simple?!

Fun Flowers

Even in the middle of winter you can have a bounty of spring flowers. Why not fold a bouquet of tulips from several sheets of paper in a rainbow of colors? You might give each flower a stem by looking at page 237.

Directions

1. Begin with a square of paper turned to form a diamond shape. Fold the paper in half and then fold over point A to meet point B. Then carefully repeat this step with the left side of the triangle, bringing point C to meet point D.

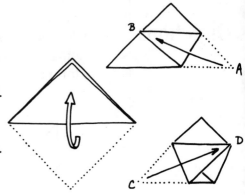

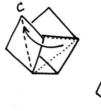

2. This is a little tricky. Lift point C up at a right angle to the form. Got that? Now push down on point C to flatten the form. Repeat this step with point A. It's easier now that you've had practice.

3. Use a mountain fold to fold back sides 1 and 2, then use a mountain fold again, but this time fold the entire form in half.

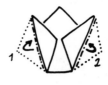

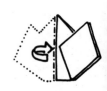

4. Fold up point E. Be sure to make a sharp crease, then unfold it. Now if you open the petals slightly and tuck in the base, your first flower is complete.

A Place for Your Posies

The origami tulip on page 236 or any origami flower will look even prettier at the tip of this stem with one slender leaf.

Directions

1. Begin with Basic Form 1, turning the open end down. Neatly fold points A and B to the center, then turn the form over and use a valley fold to fold it in half, bringing point C to meet point D.

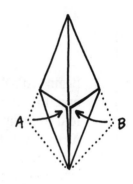

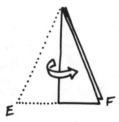

2. Use a valley fold to fold the form in half again, but this time bring point E to meet point F.

3. To complete the stem, crease the form as shown in the illustration. Then, as if you're peeling a banana, pull back on point C (back flap only) to make a delicate curved leaf.

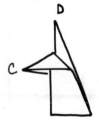

45

Funny Frog

With the help of a pair of scissors you can make this frog look real enough to hop into your heart!

Directions

1. Begin with Basic Form 4 (open end down), then use a mountain fold to bring point A back to meet point B.

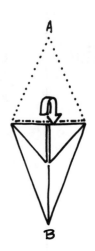

2. Next, lift point C straight up and flatten the right side of the form, then repeat this step with the left side of the form.

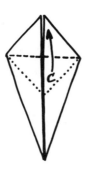

3. You've almost completed the frog's body. Fold points D and E in to the center line.

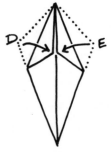

4. Using a valley fold, fold point B (front flap only) up. Then use your scissors to cut the remaining back flap from point B to a little beyond the center.

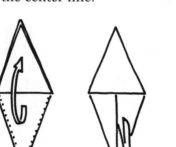

5. Next, turn your form over and carefully fold points F and G to the center.

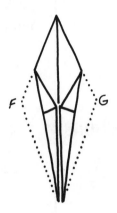

6. Are you ready to make the frog's arms and legs? Simply fold out each point as shown in the illustration.

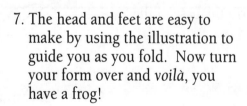

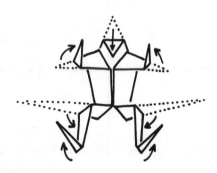

7. The head and feet are easy to make by using the illustration to guide you as you fold. Now turn your form over and *voilà*, you have a frog!

RIBBET!

46

A Clever Crustacean

You will need a pair of scissors to make this little crab.

Directions

1. Begin with Basic Form 8, then use a valley fold to fold down side 1 to meet the center line.

2. Next, take out your scissors and make four small cuts in the upper flap as shown in the illustration.

3. Now fold up the cuts to form the crab's eyes. Then fold up points A and B to form the base of the body.

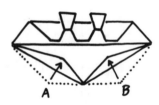

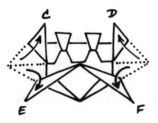

4. The legs and claws are last. Make them by folding points C, D, E, and F as shown in the illustration, then turn the form over and your crab is ready to crawl.

Plucky Paper Penguin

You can use any color of paper to make your plucky paper penguin, but to make this Antarctic bird more realistic, use black paper with a white underside and your penguin will have its proper tuxedo!

Directions

1. Begin with Basic Form 1. Use a mountain fold to fold the form in half, then fold back point A, but not quite all the way. Use the illustration as a guide. Turn the form over and repeat this step.

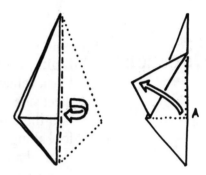

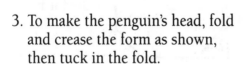

2. Now fold point A down again as shown. Turn the form over and repeat this on the other side.

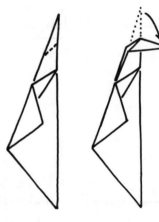

3. To make the penguin's head, fold and crease the form as shown, then tuck in the fold.

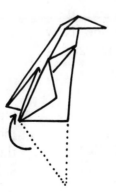

4. The penguin will stand if you make a crease at the bottom of the form as shown, then tuck the paper inside the form. Brrrrrrrr . . . your Antarctic bird is complete.

Holiday Basket

On Valentine's Day use red paper to make this charming basket and fill it with candy hearts for someone special. On Easter fill it with little candy eggs!

Directions

1. Begin with a square of paper. Use a valley fold to fold side 1 to meet side 2 so that the open end is at the top. Make a half-inch fold along one side (or greater than a half-inch if your paper is larger than usual). Crease the paper, then cut along the crease and put aside the extra piece until later.

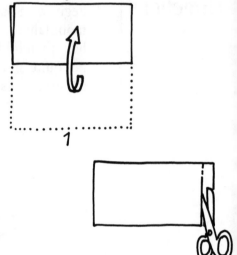

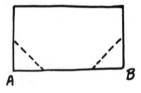

2. Fold points A and B up and back to make the creases as shown, then tuck points A and B inside the form.

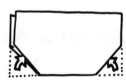

3. Using valley folds, fold sides 3 and 4 (front flap only) so that they meet at the center line. Now use mountain folds to repeat this step with the back flap.

4. Now it's time to use that extra piece of paper you set aside. Make the basket's handle by folding both sides lengthwise into the center.

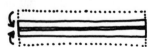

5. Slip one end into the form as shown in the illustration. Next, fold side 5 (front flap only) down twice so that the second fold is tucked into the basket.

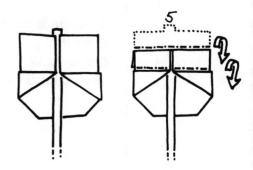

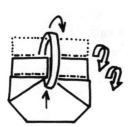

6. Here's where it gets a little tricky. Turn the basket over, lift the handle up and over, and loop it into the open flaps in the middle of the form, then repeat step 5 on this side.

7. Finally, make a sharp crease across the bottom of the form, then open the basket and flatten it at the base.

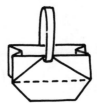

Jungle Cat

This jungle cat will be happy to sit beside you whenever you want company. Use any color paper you like, but be sure to draw on a cute face to make your cat complete. You might give it spots to make it a leopard, or turn it into a tiger with real tiger stripes!

Directions

1. Begin with Basic Form 1 (open end down), then use a valley fold to bring point A to meet point B.

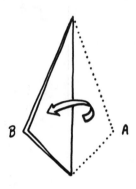

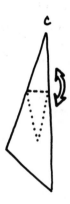

2. Fold down point C about halfway as shown in the illustration. Crease the paper sharply, then unfold it.

3. Study the drawing before you begin this next step. Now use a valley fold to fold back side 1 (front flap only) toward side 2 so that your paper is shaped like that in the illustration. The top of your form will curve slightly. When this is accomplished, fold down point C again.

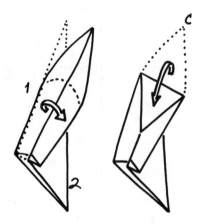

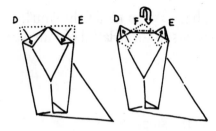

4. It's time to make the kitty's ears. First, use valley folds to fold down points D and E. Next, use a mountain fold to turn back point F. Finally, fold back points D and E again.

5. The kitty's face is a little tricky so, once again, study the illustration carefully before you begin. Find the crease at the center of the face. Place one finger a little to the left of the crease. With your other finger on the right side of the crease, push the paper to the left and flatten it as shown in the illustration. Got that? Now use a mountain fold to tuck point C under the kitty's face.

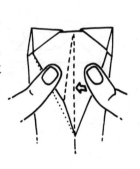

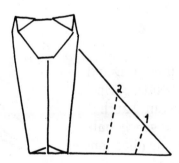

6. To make the tail, fold and unfold point G, making two sharp creases as shown. Now open the form slightly and tuck crease 1 into crease 2.

7. The final detail is to fold back sides 1 and 2 to create the kitty's slender front legs. Grrrrrrrrrrr!

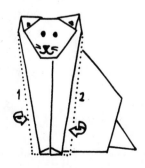

Finny Friend

When is a hat not a hat? When it's a fish! You'll see for yourself when you use a pair of scissors to turn Hatful of Fun on page 183 into this adorable angelfish.

Directions

1. Begin by following the steps to make the Hatful of Fun, but when you get to step 3, don't fold in the back flap.

2. Use your scissors to make a cut on each side of the back flap at points A and B. Each cut should be about two-thirds of the way to the center. When you are finished with this step, use a mountain fold to fold back point C.

3. Now hold the hat at point D and turn the form to the side. Grip point C (single flap only) at the back of the form and gently pull both points in opposite directions to see your fish take shape.

4. Last but not least, flatten the form and your finny friend is ready to swim.

Origami Gets Even More Original!

There are so many different things you can do with origami, it's truly amazing! In the next few pages, you'll find all sorts of ideas and uses for the origami crafts you've created—from decorating the house for a special holiday to brightening up a corner of your room. (And wait till you see the ideas on hosting your own origami party!)

Fun and Functional

Not only is origami beautiful to look at, but you can also construct some origami pieces to be used around the house or in your room.

If you have a penchant for pictures but can't afford expensive frames, make the The Great Frame Fold-Up! on page 188. You can even fold your own jewelry, such as the adorable Friendship Ring on page 212. Increase the life span of your ring by coating it with clear varnish or rubber cement.

The Cute Cup and Handy Holder (pages 206 and 207) will both prove very useful if you ever need containers for those precious "valuables," like jelly beans, pennies, or cool rocks!

Handmade Holiday Cheer

Holidays are the perfect time to create stunning handmade origami decorations for your walls and tables. Following you'll find some great ideas for bringing out the origami spirit all year long!

New Year's Eve: Create unique confetti containers on page 221 with Star Quality. To further decorate your stars use colorful markers to write in the new year that you and your friends are celebrating.

Valentine's Day: Fold a decorative gift box for that special friend, then fill it with his or her favorite candied hearts. Wrap It Up, the gift box found on page 196, can be created with red or pink paper. Or find some special Valentine's Day wrapping paper and cut it down to the size you want for your box.

Fold up the Paper Pocket on pages 219 and 220 to hold an extra-secret Valentine's message. Depending on what size of paper you use, you can make a large envelope or a small, precious one. Seal it closed with your favorite Valentine's stickers. (A piece of clear tape works, too.)

Easter: No Easter holiday is complete without the treasured Easter basket. Make your own mini-baskets (A Tisket, a Tasket on page 187), then fill them with green tissue paper and jelly beans. They're so easy, you can make one for each member of your family.

Halloween: Turn the Hot-Air Balloon on page 208 into a frightening jack-o'-lantern! Just follow the directions for the Hot-Air Balloon, using bright orange origami paper. With a black marker, fill in gruesome or goofy facial features, your choice. Then top off your pumpkin with a piece of green pipe cleaner for its stem!

Christmas: Fill your house with the spirit of this winter holiday—the decorations are easy to make and look great! Try the Paper Pine Tree on page 225, then decorate it with colorful sequins and rhinestones. Create a chorus of beautiful angels (found on page 185). You may even want to attach thin lengths of fishing line to their halos and hang them from the ceiling for an angelic ensemble.

Hanukkah: Create beautiful candles and candle holders to decorate the holiday dinner table or your bedroom. Simply fold a pair of Creative Candle Cradles (page 193) using silver or white origami paper. Next fold a pair of Clever Candles (page 195) with bright blue paper. These attractive candles and holders will complement the joyous Festival of Lights.

Room with a View

Everyone knows about painting walls or hanging wallpaper to decorate a room. But you can have a look that's all your own—your friends will beg you to show them how you did it—when you use your imagination and get down to some serious decorating with origami!

The wonderful thing about using origami figures for making your room more attractive is that you can switch colors, add to them, or take them down easily when you want a change of scenery. Here are some ideas to get you thinking:

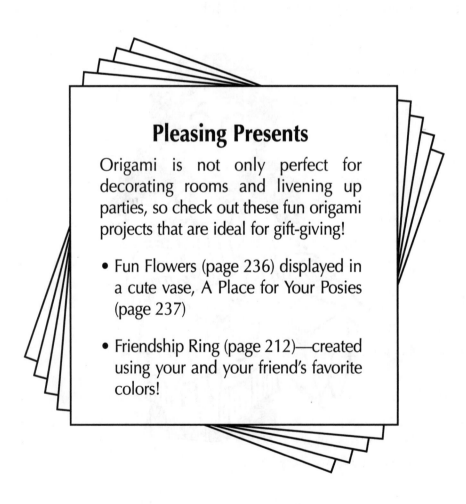

Pleasing Presents

Origami is not only perfect for decorating rooms and livening up parties, so check out these fun origami projects that are ideal for gift-giving!

- Fun Flowers (page 236) displayed in a cute vase, A Place for Your Posies (page 237)

- Friendship Ring (page 212)—created using your and your friend's favorite colors!

Pet-in-a-Bowl: Here are some pets you never have to feed! Create a few turtles (page 215) or frogs (page 238) using different green-colored paper. Find an old empty fishbowl (a glass bowl will work, too) and cover the bottom with sand, pretty rocks, or dried twigs. Stick your pets in the bowl to create a fun pond scene without the trouble of water!

I Love Cats and Dogs Mobile: To create the base for your mobile, simply take two long sticks or dowels and cross them in the middle. Secure them together with strong string or cord. Now choose your pets. You may want to pick the cute dog and cat head shapes, Precious Pup/Cuddly Kitty, found on page 202, or fold the full bodies of the pets. Sitting Pretty Puppy is found on page 235, and Jungle Cat is on page 244. Fold your origami and decorate as you wish. Then take a thin piece of string and attach it to the top of each animal shape. Tie the other end of each string to the mobile. Have an adult help you hang the mobile from the ceiling. Are the puppies chasing the kitties, or is it the other way around?

A Bounty of Birds: For this mobile you'll need a large branch with smaller branches and twigs. Choose five to eight origami birds and fold them, using the brightest origami paper you have. A variety of flying creatures can be found throughout, such as Chattering Bird (page 201), Fluttering Butterfly (page 214), and Beautiful Bird (pages 231 and 232). You may even want to add some pesky flies (page 203)! Hang a couple from the branches and stick a few among the twigs. Ask an adult to help you hang the finished craft from the ceiling.

A Day at Sea: For the nautical lover in you, fill a blank wall with an entire ocean scene. (For this project you'll need to tape or thumbtack poster board to the wall. Check with your parents for an okay first.)

To create the backdrop, you'll need both a light blue piece of poster board and a darker blue piece. Depending on how much space you have, fit the two pieces so that the light blue is on the top half for the sky and the dark blue board is just below the lighter board, representing the ocean.

Now it's your turn to get creative! Make a bright red sailboat (page 182) on the top of the ocean or a crab crawling along the ocean floor (page 240). Create a variety of colorful fish (page 246). You may even want to glue some silver sequins on them to give the illusion of shiny scales. Use the directions to make the Hot-Air Balloon (page 208) to create a bright yellow sun hanging high in the sky. Add a seal (page 217) playing in the water with a gigantic whale (page 200). In this ocean environment anything goes! Once you've created all your origami pieces, you'll want to attach fishing line to the top of each one to hang from the ceiling. Cut the lengths of line so that the boat appears to float along the top of the water, the fish look like they're swimming in the ocean, and the crab is on the floor of the ocean.

Your Day at Sea will be in constant motion as the origami pieces catch the slightest breezes and bounce and move along the waves!

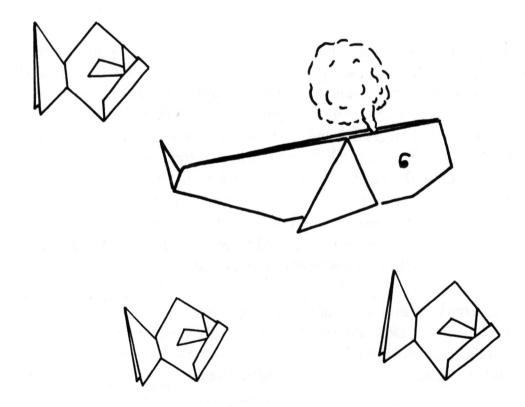

The Ultimate Origami-Rama!

Imagine a party that's totally different than any you've ever been to—an origami original! Personalize party goods by using origami for invitations, place cards, decorations, favor bags, and art projects.

Start off your party plans by making an origami invitation for each guest. Pick any origami object you like that has enough space to write the time, place, and date of your party. Or, if your friends are as crazy about origami as you are, send an unfolded sheet of origami paper with the party details. Then have each person create his or her own origami craft from the enclosed paper and bring it to the party to share. Display the origami on a bookshelf or table for all to admire.

When it comes to decorating for your party, try one of these incredible centerpieces to adorn the food and drink table or any other space you wish:

Top It Off!

Origami crafts are perfect for decorating packages. Here are some ideas to beautify and personalize your gifts:

- Rock-a-Bye Baby (page 233)—looks adorable on baby shower gifts!

- Here Comes Santa Claus! (page 234)—add your own cheerful face to this Santa head

- Let's Make Music! (page 227)—for your favorite music lover, his or her very own piano

- Fun Flowers (page 236)—always appropriate on any gift for Mom, Grandma, or that special aunt

The Ocean: Cover your table with sheets of crinkled blue tissue paper. The crinkles will give the paper an ocean wave look. Then create a Finny Friend (page 246) for each guest. Spread the cute fish around the table and invite your friends to take one home after the evening is over. On page 200 you can find out how to create a gigantic whale in A Whale of an Idea. Don't forget to stick some cotton in the large whale's spout to suggest spurting water! If you have room, create a few Super Simple Sailboats (page 182) in bright colors to complement the blue water.

In the Country: Create an outdoor centerpiece that's a sweet barnyard scene. First, sprinkle the table with hay on which you can set your origami pieces. Choose your favorite animals from this book to fill the yard, such as a pig (page 178), a hen (page 198), butterflies (page 214), a rabbit (page 229), and a couple of frogs (page 238). Don't forget to "build" a big bright red barn, too, found on page 180.

If you have time, you may want to fold up little party favors for each friend, like a beautiful basket filled with candy (page 242), a friendship ring (page 212), or a pinwheel that really spins (page 191).

At your party, supply a variety of colorful paper so all your guests can join in the paper-folding fun. Be sure to have on hand glue, glitter, and anything else that can be used to decorate your paper crafts. This will be one party that's unforgettable!

For More Information

If you just can't get enough on origami, Origami USA would love to hear from you. They are a nonprofit organization whose mission is to spread knowledge of origami as an art and a craft.

They have groups across the country, and you can find out more information about them by sending a self-addressed, stamped envelope with two first-class stamps to:

Origami USA
15 West 77th Street
New York, NY 10024-5192

Or call (212) 769-5635.

They also have a Website! Check it out at:
www.origami-usa.org